ASHE Higher Education Report: Volume 36, Number 3
Kelly Ward, Lisa E. Wolf-Wendel, Series Editors

The Global Growth of Private Higher Education

Kevin Kinser

Daniel C. Levy

Juan Carlos Silas Casillas

Andrés Bernasconi

Snejana Slantcheva-Durst

Wycliffe Otieno

Jason E. Lane

Prachayani Praphamontripong

William Zumeta

Robin LaSota

D1526720

The Global Growth of Private Higher Education

Kevin Kinser, Daniel C. Levy, Juan Carlos Silas Casillas, Andrés Bernasconi, Snejana Slantcheva-Durst, Wycliffe Otieno, Jason E. Lane, Prachayani Praphamontripong, William Zumeta, and Robin LaSota

ASHE Higher Education Report: Volume 36, Number 3
Kelly Ward, Lisa E. Wolf-Wendel, Series Editors

ISSN 1551-6970   electronic ISSN 1554-6306   ISBN 978-0-4709-2978-0

The **ASHE Higher Education Report** is part of the Jossey-Bass Higher and Adult Education Series and is published six times a year by Wiley Subscription Services, Inc., A Wiley Company, at Jossey-Bass, 989 Market Street, San Francisco, California 94103-1741.

For subscription information, see the Back Issue/Subscription Order Form in the back of this volume.

CALL FOR PROPOSALS: Prospective authors are strongly encouraged to contact Kelly Ward (kaward@wsu.edu) or Lisa Wolf-Wendel (lwolf@ku.edu). See "About the ASHE Higher Education Report Series" in the back of this volume.

Visit the Jossey-Bass Web site at **www.josseybass.com.**

Printed in the United States of America on acid-free recycled paper.

The **ASHE Higher Education Report** is indexed in CIJE: Current Index to Journals in Education (ERIC), Current Abstracts (EBSCO), Education Index/Abstracts (H.W. Wilson), ERIC Database (Education Resources Information Center), Higher Education Abstracts (Claremont Graduate University), IBR & IBZ: International Bibliographies of Periodical Literature (K.G. Saur), and Resources in Education (ERIC).

Advisory Board

The ASHE Higher Education Report Series is sponsored by the Association for the Study of Higher Education (ASHE), which provides an editorial advisory board of ASHE members.

Contents

Executive Summary

The assumption that higher education is always or primarily provided by the state has not been accurate in most countries for a very long time. In recent decades, however, private higher education has achieved global significance. The importance of the private sector can be measured in enrollment, with approximately a third of all students in attendance at tertiary levels. It can be seen in the proportion of private institutions in many countries, where they represent the clear majority. It is evident in the policy sphere, as new quality assurance mechanisms and regulatory regimes have emerged to address the specific issues raised by non-state-sponsored educational entities. And it is obvious in terms of growth, the specific subject of this volume.

This monograph is a collaboration that illuminates the diversity and distinctiveness of the sector through in-depth case studies and scholarly analysis with a global perspective. The cases were selected to provide global coverage of the growth of private higher education, drawing on the research and expertise of affiliates and collaborating scholars of the Program on Research on Private Higher Education at the University at Albany, State University of New York. The authors, having contributed themselves to the development of the literature on private higher education, are eminently suited to articulating the trends and conclusions that have become evident over the last twenty years of research in the field.

The ten authors write about private higher education in Mexico, Chile, Bulgaria, Kenya, Dubai, Thailand, and the United States. They touch as well on the essentially private function of cross-border higher education around the world. The common themes across the cases are the growth of private higher education, the multiple ways in which that growth has manifested itself, and the myriad of policy responses to the growth.

The cases provide examples of private higher education sectors that have comparatively long histories such as Chile and the United States and those with quite recent development like Bulgaria and Dubai. Across all cases, the growth of private higher education is evident, demonstrating the global reach of the phenomenon. In some cases such as Kenya and Bulgaria, after initial growth the expansion of the sector leveled off. In others such as Mexico and the for-profit sector of the United States, the growth of private higher education continues apace.

The cases also emphasize the diversity of private higher education. The three types of private higher education that the literature has long recognized—religious, elite, and demand absorbing—are joined in these cases by group or identity-based, semielite, and serious-demand-absorbing institutions. Only the elite form of private higher education does not show current growth, though the semielite form is making inroads in Thailand. Religious private higher education is growing, though typically not from the traditional Catholic identity; such is the case in Chile. Other religions as well as ethnic groups have developed their own institutions that counter the dominant state provision. By far the greatest growth is in demand-absorbing institutions, representing mostly lower-level and lower-quality institutions that cater to the surging demand for education, demand beyond the capacity of the existing system to handle. Some demand-absorbing institutions attempt seriously to improve educational quality, though others operate with limited resources and low expectations for students. The demand-absorbing conditions are most prevalent in the developing world, the majority of the cases in this volume, where demographic growth and limited public capacity intersect most clearly.

The for-profit form has also emerged, though only in the United States does it represent a significant contribution to the overall capacity among the countries reviewed. It has as well been increasing in numbers in Mexico. The form is not allowed in all countries, though in Chile the prohibition extends only to universities and not all of higher education. As an aspect of cross-border higher education, excess revenue generation is a prime motivator for institutions to establish international branch campuses, even when the form is legally nonprofit in the host country. In addition, many of the demand-absorbing forms throughout the world act much like the for-profit form, and the Thai case shows that ownership can be with a proprietor, even as the for-profit form is barred. Thus the line between profit and nonprofit can be blurred.

In most cases, the growth of private higher education is the result of either loosened government regulations or the emergence of the new form in a regulatory vacuum. Regulatory delays happen as well, when growth occurs faster and more substantially than was anticipated, resulting in policy responses to address new unanticipated concerns. The Dubai case, however, is an example of government-sponsored growth in private higher education, distinctive also in that it relies on international providers. The cross-border higher education example in Dubai shows the reliance of international branch campuses on liberalization of regulations globally; even when international branch campuses are not the dominant form of private higher education, regulatory reform and openness to the private form are necessary to the development of cross-border higher education.

A subset of the growth of private higher education is represented by the privatization of the public sector. Fee-paying students may enroll alongside subsidized students, or systems of tuition may be instituted for all students. Often it is coupled with a loan system that allows students some choice among institutions (though the United States is nearly alone in extending that loan subsidy to the for-profit subsector). A parallel phenomenon of private higher education is the dependency in some countries of the private sector on public subsidies, either through state-sponsored loan schemes or direct funding of the private sector.

The decline of private higher education after establishing a viable stake in a system of higher education has only rarely been seen, though restrictions on growth from new regulations are more common. Bulgaria and Kenya provide relevant examples of how regulations affect growth in this way, with Bulgaria serving as a historic case of change in political regime eliminating the private form on ideological grounds. A change in regime does not always lead to change in private higher education, however, as the Chilean case demonstrates.

In sum, the cases suggest both similarities and differences in the emergence of private higher education among the represented countries. They collectively provide a key brief on the status of private higher education scholarship in the world today.

Foreword

This monograph comes out of the Program for Research on Private Higher Education (PROPHE) based at the University at Albany, State University of New York. Monograph coauthor Daniel Levy is the organizer and coordinator of a global network of scholars who seek to build knowledge about private higher education around the world. Over the last decade, the PROPHE has sponsored a series of working papers on private higher education, produced or coproduced regionally based volumes, and presented original research at numerous conferences, including the Association for the Study of Higher Education. (A list of working papers and other research activity is available online at the PROPHE website, http://www.albany.edu/dept/eaps/prophe/). The idea for this volume emerged from an ongoing conversation in the PROPHE about how best to disseminate the collective scholarly work generated in and through the network. A serendipitous conversation between series editor Lisa Wolf-Wendel and lead author Kevin Kinser suggested the ASHE monograph series as an appropriate venue.

PROPHE collaborating scholars and other PROPHE contributors were recruited to provide global coverage of the private higher education phenomenon. Each author took the lead for composing a case analysis based on the private higher education literature, his or her own research, and personal knowledge of local history and contexts. The goal was to approach the topic of private higher education inductively, from the specific to the general, rather than introducing broad themes and then providing individual cases for examples.

The format of this volume is somewhat unusual for the series. The introduction and final chapter in the monograph identify overarching themes and perspectives, with the chapters in the middle serving as source data and primary analysis of private growth in each case. The sequence of chapters is intended only to provide a logical geographic progression from Latin America to Europe, Africa, the Middle East, Asia, and finally to North America, with the cross-border overview representing the last case. It is possible, therefore, to read each case chapter as a stand-alone case study, though each references the others—not just in specific details but also in the prior scholarship of authors as leading scholars in the field.

The subject of the monograph is also unusual for the series in that it addresses a topic of international concern without immediate parallels in the United States. For U.S. readers lacking an international focus, the topic may seem odd, as private higher education is neither new nor controversial in this country, nor has it recently had growth as a key issue. Still, the themes of growth in private higher education and resultant policy responses resonate through the large and recent expansion of the for-profit sector. The U.S. case in the volume is therefore included to emphasize the for-profit dimension. This emphasis demonstrates the importance of the comparative approach, where understanding an issue in its global complexity provides new knowledge applicable to the local case.

This volume makes several contributions to the existing literature private higher education. First, it brings together in one volume the most substantial analysis of the growth of global private higher education yet attempted. Other book-length works have tackled growth as one element among many issues relevant to the private higher education phenomenon, and numerous articles and case studies have amply documented the case for growth and attendant policy responses in various countries and regions. Indeed, many of these works were written by this volume's authors. The effort here is notable for its comprehensive approach.

Second, the authors provide summative analyses of private higher education in a range of countries that go beyond typical case descriptions. The authors document the history, context, and current dimensions of private higher education in each case, with explicit reference to regional and global trends. The specific characteristics of the cases define how they are presented so that the most salient features of the private higher education phenomenon are highlighted.

Third, the monograph does more than recount the literature as it exists. The authors extend previous work on multiple fronts by developing various new data sources and analyses, new conceptual frameworks, new classifications and categorizations, and new examples of previously identified private higher education phenomena.

Fourth, the literature on private higher education is often published in specialized or regional outlets that reflect the more narrow interest of their audience. This monograph is written for a general audience of higher education scholars, practitioners, and policymakers.

Finally, the volume represents a significant attempt to engage broadly in a topic with global significance by taking advantage of a multiauthor collaboration. Thus, the topic can be addressed from several angles while being neither too general nor too laden with details.

In sum, this monograph provides a coherent picture of a complicated subject. The growth of private higher education is important in nearly every region of the world. This effort emphasizes the importance of rigorous scholarship in understanding the topic and addressing its ongoing influence on higher education systems in the United States and abroad.

Published online in Wiley Online Library
(wileyonlinelibrary.com) • DOI: 10.1002/aehe.3603

Introduction

IN THE RISING GLOBAL LITERATURE on private higher education, no topic has been more discussed than growth. One should pay attention to several relevant strands of growth. In countries where only a few years ago the private sector was a marginal entity in higher education, now a significant proportion of overall enrollment is claimed by private higher education. Great numbers of private institutions have emerged to meet the demand for education, demand that the public sector is unable or unwilling to meet. New institutional forms of education, too, have come into existence in many countries, sponsored by a range of entities, including individual proprietors, profit-seeking business interests, charitable organizations, and cultural foundations. Private sector subjects include not only lower-level skills and technical training but also graduate degrees in business and other fields important for economic development. And in addition to domestic provision, private higher education in dozens of countries now involves new international branch campuses and foreign investment and ownership of local institutions.

As diverse as the forms of growth are that have captured attention, the literature itself can be lacking in comparative perspective. To be sure, the growth of private higher education is not an isolated phenomenon. The scope of private higher education expansion demands a global awareness of trends and an understanding of the theoretical frames that have demonstrated explanatory power. Certainly, several single-author studies and edited volumes have global

The primary responsibility for developing this chapter was taken by Kevin Kinser.

The Global Growth of Private Higher Education   1

breadth and analysis, including regional scope and variation (Levy, 1986; Mabizela, Levy, and Otieno, 2007; Slantcheva and Levy, 2007). Others have focused on global trends in particular subsectors (see, for example, Kinser, 2010; Kinser and Levy, 2006). Yet until now, no volume has brought together individual national case studies of the growth in private higher education grounded in the established literature of private higher education, with an explicitly global focus. Moreover, this volume's chapters include regional scope and subsector awareness in the national cases, tied up and expanded by a global concluding chapter.

The national case detail found in this volume can be found in no other source. Each author is an expert on private higher education in one of the case countries, indeed on its higher education system overall. At the same time—and quite unlike the reality in the great majority of country treatments of private higher education—each author in this volume knows the established literature on private higher education internationally. The chapters are not merely isolated descriptive case studies. Rather, they form the most current illumination of the history, context, trends, and policy debates surrounding private higher education as it exists in the world today.

Significance of Private Higher Education

As enticing as expansion of private higher education may be, the fundamental existence of a private sector has global significance that deserves attention in its own right. It is noteworthy that in much of the world, many consider higher education the responsibility of the state. Policy and practice have historically neglected the private provision of higher education, with nonstate institutions suffering from questions of legitimacy and seen as marginal to the education of the citizenry. The public sector, on the other hand, is often the apex of the educational system and preferred by students and policymakers alike. Among the few exceptions to the dominant position of public sector higher education is the distracting example of the United States, which has had from the beginning a strong and educationally significant private educational sector, and many Latin American countries that for at least a half century have shown preferences for private higher education in an array of fields.

In any case, the fact that private higher education is now substantially contributing to the global educational capacity is not an obvious outcome.

Scholars have identified three basic conditions that do much to explain the development of private higher education in a public sector–dominant system of higher education (Geiger, 1986; Levy, 1986). First, private institutions may offer something different from the public sector, whether through a special curriculum, a particular religious or cultural emphasis, or some other way to distinguish themselves from the public sector. Second, the private sector can provide something better to public sector alternatives by ratcheting up quality of the education, often accompanied by stricter admission standards. Finally, the private option may serve additional students who find the public system closed to them because of capacity or geographic constraints.

The first condition suggests the "old" private higher education institutions that have existed in many countries for decades. The Chilean case in this volume as well as the colonial and antebellum history of higher education in the United States provide good examples. Religious institutions, for example, may provide largely secular education to adherents of the faith. Minority or majority ethnic groups may establish a private institution with a mission to maintain and promulgate their identity or language as a distinctive cultural marker. These institutions have long been around, yet the surge in private higher education overall has nonetheless included this category as well, especially in countries where new openness to the private provision has loosened monolithic government controls over minorities or religious groups.

The second condition also recognizes some of the older private schools, though the existence of an elite private sector is both historically and currently rare outside the United States. More recently, the notion of a semielite private sector has emerged (Levy, 2008a) to describe the serious intentions and status of a subset of institutions in some countries. The Thai case in this volume provides good examples of this phenomenon as it fits the theme of growth in private higher education. Another aspect of it is seen in the burgeoning cross-border higher education trend of establishing international branch campuses with specific goals of raising the bar for local institutions. Dubai provides a specific example of this phenomenon as well as being noted as an illustration of the growth of private higher education.

But by far the greatest expansion globally has been the growing demand for education and the ability of private higher education to serve students who have limited access to existing institutions. The short-hand expression coined for the new institutions that have emerged is "demand-absorbing" (Levy, 1986), suggesting private higher education's sponge-like ability to soak up the pool of remaining students who do not otherwise find places in the system. Here not only is the growth, but also the concentration of concern from policy-makers the greatest. This expansion represented in many areas an unanticipated development (Levy, 2006) that occurred in a policy vacuum. As demand-absorbing private higher education largely lacked rules of the road at its onset, on-the-ground reality often took precedence over what was legal or approved. All the countries profiled here experienced versions of this situation, with evident and ongoing consequences. Even now, regulatory activity varies, and quality assurance and accreditation issues remain unresolved in many places.

In short, then, the significance of private higher education rests often with its distinctiveness compared with much of the public sector. But also one should recognize the sector's diversity based on local factors governing its emergence as well as the various policy responses engendered during development. The cases in this volume reflect these dimensions, even as the theme of the volume sits squarely on the matter of growth and expansion.

Choosing the Cases

The cases were chosen with the first goal of providing global coverage of the growth in private higher education and attendant issues and the second goal of ensuring that knowledgeable authority could be brought to bear on individual cases. To meet the first goal, the cases must circle the world, touching North America, Latin America, Europe, the Middle East, Africa, and Asia. Global coverage was further extended through the inclusion of a survey chapter covering trends and issues associated with the growth of cross-border higher education.

Within these geographic groupings, though, the choice of countries more reflected our second goal. The authors of this volume have been working together for much of the last decade to build knowledge about private higher education around the world. Organized primarily through the University at Albany's Program for Research On Private Higher Education (PROPHE), and led by coauthor Daniel Levy, the authors are scholars not just of private higher education in a particular country but also of the broader private higher education literature and the comparative analyses made possible through the PROPHE's long-term collaborative efforts. For this volume, then, the cases focus on the expertise developed in the PROPHE network, tapping into each author's expertise in a country, with regional and global trends drawn from the literature and the collective knowledge of the group.

The specific countries chosen, therefore, should not be seen as representative of their region. Nor are they necessarily typical exemplars of particular features of the growth in private higher education. They are, however, significant cases that suggest the diversity and distinctiveness of the phenomenon as it has been experienced around the world. And perhaps as important, they are indicative of the scholarly direction and conceptual focus of the current literature on private higher education. Thus, the cases together with the concluding chapter provide a primer for global private higher education scholarship as it exists today.

Organization of the Volume

After this introductory chapter, the volume begins its global tour with the case of Mexico, with key authorship by Juan Carlos Silas Casillas. The Mexican case is significant because of its original importance in defining the primary types of private higher education (Levy, 1986). It shows trends that reflect rapid transformations in the country and tensions in developing countries at the intersection of resource constraints, relatively weak regulations, and educational demand.

Chile forms the next case, with Andrés Bernasconi as key author. The South American country exhibits what might be termed a private dominant higher education system, with an arguably elite core, some of it with operational support from the government. Privatization is a dominant theme, as all institutions, public and private, increasingly rely on nongovernmental sources of income.

The third case presents Bulgaria, with key authorship by Snejana Slantcheva-Durst. As part of postcommunist Europe, Bulgaria shows the swift development of a private sector, the regulatory responses, and responses of the public sector to new competition. Significant also is the challenge of regional harmonization with a still largely public-oriented European Union educational system.

Next the volume turns to Africa and the case of Kenya, with Wycliffe Otieno as key author. In Kenya the initial expansion is countered by a strong public sector response as well as a toughened regulatory scheme that resulted in slower enrollment growth in private higher education than elsewhere. The resilience of public privilege is emphasized.

The chapter on Dubai follows, with key authorship by Jason Lane. The newest entry into the private higher education universe, the emirate has followed a specific path of government-sanctioned expansion led by international branch campuses organized into free-trade zones. Demand is from the expatriate community and demonstrates a role of private higher education in establishing educational hubs.

The case of Thailand, key authorship by Prachayani Praphamontripong, is the sixth example in the volume. The country shows the diversity of private provision as well as the role of regulations in managing expansion and loan-financed tuition plans. The Thai case also emphasizes patterns of expansion and stagnation in reaction to policies and national instability.

The U.S. case, with William Zumeta and Robin LaSota as key authors, presents a subsector focus on growth, where for-profit growth has been the dominant source of expansion. The more traditional nonprofit institutions have adjusted their target student populations and adjusted curricula to reflect the changing and competitive market for higher education.

The last case in the volume is that of cross-border higher education, with key authorship by Kevin Kinser. The global survey of cross-border activity is included not only because its quick growth mimics trends seen in private higher education but also because private sector regulations are key to how host countries welcome or restrict foreign activity in their borders. The chapter suggests the plasticity of borders in an increasingly mobile world and the limitations of national models on transnational institutions.

The volume concludes with a chapter reflecting on the global growth of higher education, with Daniel Levy as key author. Inspired both by the cases herein as well as other examples drawn from the wider private higher education literature, the concluding chapter suggests the trends and regional variations that explain the growth in private higher education and the diversity and distinctiveness of various models and institutional patterns. Speculation about the decline of private higher education is included as an additional complicating factor to explaining global growth patterns.

The Growth of the Private Sector in Mexican Higher Education

MEXICO HAS EXPERIENCED A RAPID TRANSITION in its economical, social, cultural, and educational development, changing from rural to urban, from a lack of industry to a technically industrialized country, and lately from a very young and rapidly growing population to a society that has slowed its demographic growth and started to age. In the educational realm, Mexico portrays many of the tensions faced by developing countries—exponential growth at all educational levels, perceived decline in the quality of education, and virtual stagnation of financial support.

Trends in the Higher Education System in Mexico

Demographic, social, and political changes have resulted in three basic trends in Mexican higher education: strong growth in enrollment of the higher education system as a whole; substantial diversification, meaning the emergence of various types of institutions with alternative programs and delivery modes; and a significant increase in the number of private institutions and their share of the national enrollment.

The first trend—dynamic growth in the enrollment of the higher education system as a whole—seems to be the result of aggressive policies for expansion nationwide. The national enrollment in basic education (K–9) went from 10,750,545 students in 1970–1971 to 25,516,150 in 2007–2008, or about

The primary responsibility for developing this chapter was taken by Juan Carlos Silas Casillas.

389,000 new children each year. High school enrollment went from 369,299 students in 1970 to 3,830,042 in 2007–2008, or an average of 91,072 new students each year. In higher education, the situation is outstanding, especially in the *licenciatura* level, the emblematic higher education degree, because it has grown from 252,236 students in 1970–1971 to 2,317,001 in 2007–2008, which represents an annual growth of 24 percent. The expansion in enrollment is also evident in the construction (or refurbishing of schools) and hiring of teaching personnel.

The second trend is the diversification of institutions, delivery modes, and academic programs. It is related to the enrollment increase and is affected by an apparent paradigm shift about the advantages and outcomes of higher education. The main changes are the development of new market-oriented programs in existing public and private institutions and the start of new institutions aimed to respond to the educational (vocational training) needs of professionals in the job market.

The late 1980s and 1990s were particularly distinctive on these issues. Higher education institutions included new disciplines, mostly related to computer science, media communication, and industrial production, while programs such as agronomy or marine sciences and primary sector related programs decreased significantly (Asociación Nacional de Universidades e Instituciones de Educación Superior, 2003b). In addition, nonuniversity higher education institutions mushroomed in both private and public scenarios. Nonuniversity institutions have a highly specialized disciplinary focus and do not have teaching as a core activity but offer some *licenciatura* or graduate degrees. In the private realm, these organizations have programs focused on a particular field (communication sciences, psychology and psychotherapy, dentistry, or gastronomy) and are smaller in size, usually created by families or individual entrepreneurs whose geographical coverage is circumscribed to a specific urban area. They offer programs usually related with the service sector of the economy, at a very low cost of operation and very accommodating conditions for class work. Enrollment in these institutions has increased exponentially, and, according to current projections, the trend is expected to continue.

Diversification is also evident as other types of higher education have appeared, like the two-year degrees *Profesional Asociado* or *Técnico Superior*

Universitario (TSU). The creation of TSU has been recognized as a mechanism for coupling higher education formation with market needs, expecting that technological universities could contribute to the formation of the national human capital, give more options to students who want to continue their studies, and widen the work potential of citizens in underdeveloped economic regions (Villa and Flores-Crespo, 2002).

The third trend, the increase in number of private institutions and their share of the national enrollment, is related to the diversification mentioned above. Statistics from the Ministry of Education (Secretaría de Educación Pública, 2008) show a dramatic increase in enrollment in private institutions. The national total enrollment for private institutions went from 35,160 students in the 1970–1971 school year to 748,935 in 2007–2008, a 2,030 percent growth in thirty-eight years. Taking the available data from the last eighteen years (1990–2008), the total growth in the public subsystem was 669,135 students, compared with 550,728 students in the private subsystem, for a combined total of 1,219,863 new students during this period. Moreover, nearly half (45.1 percent) of these new students enrolled in the private sector.

This strong increase in both public and private sectors has several explanations, but the most important is the tacit inability of public institutions to absorb the huge demand in their classrooms. Despite titanic efforts and the creation of more spaces, growth has evident physical and economic limits. Some sort of "academic entrepreneurship" therefore aims to supply educational services to satisfy a strong social demand that has not been covered by the existing institutions. This gap seems to be tolerated or not adverted by federal and local policymakers (Levy, 2002), as the creation of nonuniversity higher education institutions has been the most common way of development of private education in the world (Kinser and Levy, 2005). This expansion seems to be known, and sometimes advocated, by national governments as well as educational systems, because it enhances the chances of low-income students to enroll in higher education.

A detailed analysis of statistics over the thirty-four years from 1970 to 2004 (Silas Casillas, 2005) showed how the private expansion experienced only two moments of decline: the 1982–1983 and 1987–1988 school years, which were characterized by economical crises that affected the purchasing power of families. During 1994–1995, the most recent Mexican economical crisis, however, national private enrollment grew by nearly 17,000 students. The remarkable situation in the 1990s is the result of an impressive expansion of low-cost private institutions, which was obviously attractive to many college students and their families.

Frameworks for the Explanation of Growth in Mexico's Private Higher Education

In the last decade of the twentieth century, scholars and policymakers noted the impressive expansion of private higher education and looked for ways to get a deeper understanding of the forces behind its growth. Demographic and budgetary issues are frequently mentioned as two explanations, while other aspects related to the operation of public institutions or the attractiveness of their delivery modes are seldom mentioned.

It has been clear since the first studies in the field (Levy, 1986) that Mexico underwent a demographic expansion during most of the twentieth century. The explosive growth added pressure to public policies and fiscal resources devoted to subjects like health, employment, and education. Children who were born at the end of the first half of the past century by the 1960s and 1970s required available spots for attending all levels of education. During these decades, national enrollments in Latin America expanded at a fairly accelerated pace. Local and national governments tried to accommodate the demand in two main ways: charter more higher education institutions (Mexico chartered twelve state universities in the 1950s, five in the 1960s, and eight in the 1970s) and look for mechanisms to enhance the student intake at the existing universities. Both options had a positive impact in the numerical sphere, but among the secondary effects one could find crowded classrooms, the accelerated hiring of ill-prepared or inexperienced teachers, and the funneling of resources into operation and "classroom issues," setting aside other important functions of academe. In this sense, massive education has had at least two known effects. First, it stresses the operation of public institutions in both the administrative-operational and the academic fields. Second, under the premise that higher education has been relevant for the social improvement of a narrow elite, lower socioeconomic groups demand a spot for studying with the expectation that it will provide them with the opportunities for social and economical progress. In general, it is reasonable to state that public universities, in the interest of amplifying the intake of students, admitted cohorts with very heterogeneous academic preparation that can be described as "below expectations."

Levy's perspective of wave one (Catholic universities), wave two (elite universities), and wave three (demand-absorbing institutions), permits a smooth analysis of the current situation in Mexico's private higher education. First-wave institutions did not appear in Mexico as a response to a bad service or as the alternative to a perception of declining quality. They started mainly because religious leaders pursue the objective of "forming youth in the religious values" at all school levels and seize the opportunity to establish higher education institutions. Following the same idea, these institutions' rhetoric about growth in enrollment and infrastructure relates more to the concept of accomplishing their evangelical mission than achieving efficiency in their operation or solid financial status.

Elite institutions, or second-wave institutions, are emblematic in Mexican private higher education. Some have international recognition, and most of them play active roles in influencing public opinion. According to Levy (1986), these institutions arose mainly as the response to the perception of declining quality of public institutions and their failure to serve as a factor of social differentiation. Affluent groups created or financed the creation of such institutions as an alternative to public education.

Third-wave institutions, better known as "demand-absorbing" institutions, focus on providing schooling opportunities to diverse groups such as low socioeconomic status college-age students or young adults who are already working but did not have the opportunity to attend college at the expected age (eighteen to twenty-three years). Based on demographic data and information about higher education, it is evident that the demand has been unsatisfied for decades and that public, religious, and elite universities do not have the financial, infrastructural, or academic capacity to take on the mission of satisfying such a huge demand.

Balán and Garcia de Fanelli (1997) created a variation of Levy's typology (1986) and argued that private higher education can be split in two groups: consolidated/elite universities and independent institutions. The first category is used to describe the big universities and technological institutes that appeared in Mexico from the 1930s to 1960s. These institutions are those that enroll more than fifteen hundred students and have full-time faculty and advanced infrastructure. Less than 90 percent of their income depends on student fees, and they have restrictive admission policies. In contrast, Balán and Garcia de Fanelli (1997) characterize independent institutions as mainly depending on students' fees and offering vocational programs oriented toward the service sector (accountancy, administration, education). These institutions are attractive to students looking for a rapid insertion in the job market.

The Demand-Absorbing Subsector as a Powerful Engine of Private Growth

Rapid growth in the number of demand-absorbing institutions and their share of national enrollment seems to correspond with the situation in many other developing countries such as India, the Philippines, Turkey, Russia, and China. This phenomenon can be partially explained by the apparent national need for providing academic credentials to the population, the unalterable need for providing new generations with higher education, and the tacit governmental incapacity for financing such activities beyond its current levels.

Two additional factors for the Mexican case are economic instability and the "shrinkage" of the economically affluent group. During the 1980s and 1990s, it is noticeable that elite and religious universities depended on economic, social, and political stability for growth and development; but recurrent crises have interfered. It has been exactly in these two decades and the first years of the twenty-first century when demand-absorbing institutions have been consistently gaining visibility in such a way that they currently represent more than half the private enrollment in Mexico. On the second factor, the Mexican high-income echelon is not growing, limiting with it the possibility for an important expansion in the enrollment of elite and religious institutions. In this sense, it seems as though first- and second-wave institutions, to increase or keep their current enrollment levels, have to direct their attention to societal groups originally outside their scope: less affluent groups and students from not-overtly-religious backgrounds. To do so, elite institutions will have to offer scholarships and support for lower-income but higher-performance students; thus, institutions from the three waves are actively recruiting middle-class, high-performance students.

Nowadays, private education in Mexico accounts for 13.5 percent of the whole national enrollment (the sum of all levels), which represents about 4.5 million students. Two interesting trends are apparent. The first is that the private enrollment share in *educación secundaria* and the two modes of higher education (*professional técnico* and *bachillerato*) is declining. This situation is mainly the result of a sustained effort by the ministry of education and the state boards to funnel important sums of money to follow the growth in the current demographic peak and the federal government's interest in responding to the World Bank's recommendation to invest budgetary money principally in primary and secondary education (Maldonado, 2002). The second trend is the already mentioned growth in the participation of private enrollment in undergraduate and graduate education, especially in the 1990s and 2000s. This phenomenon could be partially explained by the fact that during the 1990s Mexico's private higher education experienced an important growth on the number of demand-absorbing institutions that offered inexpensive postsecondary education. Arguably, one of the reasons behind the growth is that these institutions play a complementary role in providing low-cost schooling opportunities beyond public universities' limited capacity. These institutions offer relatively affordable undergraduate programs relevant to service sectors (accounting, marketing, and business) and provide educational opportunities to low-income students who have not been accepted in public institutions (because of limited available slots) yet still wish to pursue undergraduate education. In this sense, demand-absorbing institutions, despite their many weaknesses, are allowed to exist because authorities see their operation as "free help" in accomplishing their duty of providing educational opportunities to nonaffluent citizens.

Additional Frameworks for Analyzing Demand-Absorbing Institutions

One way to analyze demand-absorbing institutions and at the same time to differentiate between the academically sound institutions and the ones that are not seeking upward status is through a classification based on the number and types of accreditations they have (Silas Casillas, 2005). This approach yields a three-tier taxonomy—high profile, midprofile, and low profile—which provides a different perspective for analysis. The first category corresponds to the classically labeled elite subsector and groups of institutions having two or more accreditations (for example, SACS, ANUIES, FIMPES, or COPAES), the second category groups institutions having only one of these accreditations, and the third is closely related to the demand-absorbing division and groups of unaccredited institutions. Table 1 shows the changes in growth of enrollment in five years.

It is evident that the low-profile segment is gaining ground in both net number of students and the percentage they represent. In five years, the low-profile segment grew from 43.2 percent to 52.1 percent of total enrollment, while high-profile institutions saw a decrease in their private market share of about 3.3 percent and midprofile showed a small increase, from 13.7 percent to 15.2 percent. The three groups, with the exception of the high-profile group in 2004–2005, had important growth in their enrollment. Notable is the increase in the low-profile segment at a pace of about 38,000 new students each year, which compared with the other two segments looks remarkably strong. Not only is their slice of the pie growing, but so is the pie itself.

Additionally, the former undersecretary of higher education and scientific research (SESIC in Spanish), now undersecretary of higher education, compiled data confirming this trend (SESIC, 2004). In the section about private higher education, the SESIC divides private institutions in two subgroups: private universities and other higher education institutions (institutions that do not match the criteria to be considered full-fledged universities in terms of number of programs, areas of knowledge the programs cover, characteristics of faculty, and infrastructure, among other) (Secretaría de Educación Pública, 2000). The first notable fact of this document is that enrollment in private institutions grew more strongly than in public institutions (340,126 new students in public higher education institutions and 431,391 in private higher education institutions), representing about 91,000 more students in private institutions. The second notable aspect is that the subgroup of other higher education institutions grew markedly in both proportional terms and

TABLE 1
Private Undergraduate Enrollment in Mexico by Type of Profile

Type of Institution	Enrollment 2000–2001	Percent	Enrollment 2001–2002	Percent	Enrollment 2002–2003	Percent	Enrollment 2004–2005	Percent
High Profile	214,200	43.1	220,542	39.1	229,816	37.0	213,500	32.6
Midprofile	67,835	13.7	79,463	14.1	89,068	14.3	99,749	15.2
Low Profile	214,696	43.2	264,257	46.8	302,654	48.7	340,694	52.1
Total	496,731	100.0	564,262	100.0	621,538	100.0	654,356	100.0

Source: Asociación Nacional de Universidades e Instituciones de Educación Superior, 2001, 2002, 2003a, 2006.

gross numbers. Although the subgroup of private institutions (representing mainly the big, elite, consolidated universities) had an enrollment increment of about 209,000 students in fourteen years (from 133,132 in 1989–1990 to 342,101 in 2002–2003), other higher education institutions closely related to demand-absorbing, low-profile institutions had a stronger growth, 222,422 students, in the same fourteen years (from 53,568 in 1989–1990 to 275,990 in 2002–2003). In round numbers, public institutions expanded their enrollment by 24,000 students each year, and private institutions opened spaces for 31,000 new students, 15,900 of them enrolled in other higher education institutions.

Today in Mexico about 340,000 students seek degrees from low-profile, demand-absorbing institutions. These institutions complement public and elite universities' role of providing opportunities for college goers. These institutions present an interesting dilemma. On the one hand, they provide low-income students with opportunities to get credentials and join the job market, increasing their chances to climb the socioeconomic ladder (one of the promises made by Latin American public universities). On the other hand, these institutions have no accreditation whatsoever and no reputation for providing high-quality education. In other words, students may get the credentials but not receive a good enough education to prepare them for their professional future. Demand-absorbing institutions should, however, provide educational opportunities to segments of the society who otherwise would not have the chance to attend postsecondary education and at the same time offer vocational education that prepares their students to perform in operational positions in the industry or the tertiary sector of the economy.

Taking the positive view, one can believe that all players win. Modest-income students have the opportunity to pursue postsecondary education without the risk of not being accepted into a public institution because of the limited number of slots. If students do not make it in their first attempt, they usually give up and join the job market with a high school education and accept the salary and promotion implications. Low-profile "entrepreneurial" institutions accomplish their goals with regard to economic survival and positively affect their surrounding communities and the socioeconomic groups they targeted. National and state governments can increase the nominal educational achievement of the population without significant effort. The only actors that could possibly lose are the public institutions and the elite-consolidated private ones—although the former would not have much room anyway for accommodating the additional demand and the latter do not usually target underprivileged societal groups because they focus on different niches. In this sense, it is reasonable to draw the conclusion that low-profile or demand-absorbing institutions take the roles and functions that public institutions cannot attend and the sectors consolidated institutions leave unattended.

All in all, it is reasonable to support the idea that low-profile, demand-absorbing institutions play a crucial role in the rapid expansion of post-secondary enrollment in Mexico. This trend has implications in the social, economic, and academic spheres and could affect public policy. Because low-profile institutions focus on historically underprivileged groups and provide them with educational opportunities with a clear vocational component, they tend to play the role and wave the flag of promoters of social equity. This apparently positive situation has academic implications for the fact that professionals holding a degree from these institutions most likely will join the job market (if they are not already working) with modest preparation and expectations. Low-profile institutions, most likely, will continue focusing on providing their students with the minimum necessary in terms of knowledge and vocational skills at the most affordable price. This factor is very compelling for modest-income students who want or need the credentials to join the job market, but in the long term it may have negative consequences in terms of opening possibilities for more advanced academic attainment.

Public Policy Surrounding Private Higher Education

The existence of different types of institutions, delivery modes, and programs presents an interesting challenge to policymakers. In Mexico the regulation of private higher education institutions has been partial and discretionary in its application. A private institution can legally operate in one of four basic ways:

(1) obtain the *Registro de Validez Oficial de Estudios* (RVOE) from the ministry of education to operate nationally, (2) obtain the RVOE from the state board where the institution wants to operate, (3) obtain the *incorporación* or licensure from one of the big federal higher education institutions, or (4) obtain the *incorporación* or licensure from the flagship university of the state where the institution wants to operate. Despite the obvious differences in terms of procedures and timing, the four options present about the same difficulty and the same requisites. The core of the four options responds to the *Acuerdo 279*, which sets the requisites and procedures for obtaining the RVOE and was made official on July 10, 2000, in accordance with other regulations such as the third article of the constitution, the general law of education, or the law for the coordination of higher education.

The *Acuerdo 279* clarifies the regulation through which private petitioners may obtain the RVOE but does not make it more stringent. Requisites for paperwork and coordination of supervision are not complicated to address, which leads to a tacit streamlining of processes for right- and wrongdoers. The road in this realm seems to be uphill, as the problems of the current system are generally agreed upon but no consensus has been reached regarding corrections. Developments in this subject are yet to be seen and are not likely to happen soon.

Final Ideas

Private higher education in general and Mexican private higher education in particular remain a challenge because of their constant growth and malleability. Empirical evidence shows the importance of demand-absorbing, low-profile institutions because they account for a large and growing part of private enrollment. Demand-absorbing institutions then need deeper analyses, which should be systemic and must take into consideration the other parts of the private subsystem and the system as a whole.

The Mexican case exemplifies the tensions provoked by the lack of resources that can be allocated in public education, the large (and ever-growing) demand, and the lax regulation in place. The result of this combination of factors seems to be a tacit acceptance of the fact that public institutions will be an option for students with time to spare and a good academic record, elite institutions will be mainly an option for students coming from well-off families (independent of their academic record), and demand-absorbing institutions will be the dominant—if not the only—option for working-class students with an average academic record or bypassed students who have economic responsibilities.

Chile's Dominant Private Higher Education

THE DEVELOPMENT OF PRIVATE HIGHER EDUCATION in Chile both confirms and departs from common features of private higher education worldwide. On the one hand, as was generally the case in Latin America, historically private higher education emerged from the efforts of the Catholic church or local philanthropists to offer higher education with a particular flavor. Thereafter, private higher education in Chile is marked, as in most of the world, by a rapid expansion made possible by high demand and a favorable regulatory environment. The explosion of private higher education in the early 1990s was soon followed by a tightening of licensing requirements, which practically sealed off the entrance of new providers and caused the closing of numerous small and financially strapped institutions.

On the other hand, private higher education in Chile is comparatively older, larger, more functionally diverse, less differentiated with regard to the public sector, and more prestigious than is generally the case elsewhere. The motif of public failure as a catalyst for private growth has not been so powerful a factor as in other parts of Latin America or in Africa, for instance. Financial arrangements are highly idiosyncratic to the outside observer: nine private universities, including six affiliated with the Catholic church, receive operational subsidies from the government, while the rest fund themselves basically through tuition, but the level of public funding, for both public and private universities, ranks in proportion to the size of Chile's economy among the lowest in the world.

The primary responsibility for developing this chapter was taken by Andrés Bernasconi.

A discussion of private higher education in Chile also needs to take into account the second meaning of the concept "privatization," namely, the increasing reliance on private sources of funding in private and public institutions alike. Chile is a world leader in the proportion of private institutions of higher education, in the share of private enrollments, and in private funding of higher education. Moreover, most universities at the apex of the pyramid of prestige are private. From this perspective, it can be argued that Chile's higher education system is dominantly private, unlike practically all higher education in the world save for east Asia (Goodman and Yonezawa, 2007, pp. 443–445).

The first section of this chapter provides the historical context for present-day higher education in Chile; it is followed by discussion of patterns of growth, evolution of the regulatory framework, and a comparison of the distinctiveness of private higher education to the Chilean public system. The last section is devoted to the contemporary policy debate surrounding private higher education and what it intimates about the future of the sector.

Historical Background: From the Teaching State to Freedom of Teaching

The first thing that strikes the observer about Chile's higher education in historical perspective is the extent of its privateness. By 1980 six of the eight universities in the country were private. This fact should not be taken as evidence of private dominance, though. First, private universities were smaller: they collectively enrolled only 37 percent of students (Brunner, 1986, p. 49). Second, and most important, as Levy (1986, pp. 66–76) has argued, since the creation in 1842 of the University of Chile, the history of higher education in Chile was dominated by the state, even after private universities began to emerge toward the end of the nineteenth century and beginning of the twentieth. The concept of the "teaching state" encapsulates the notion, largely unchallenged until the last quarter of the twentieth century, that education was the state's responsibility and that private entities engaged in education were collaborators with the educational mission and function of the state. In practice, for the private universities established since the Catholic University's foundation in 1888, it meant that their students had to take examinations before commissions of professors of the University of Chile until well into the 1950s. On the other hand, it also translated into public financial support for private universities. These factors, together with the small size of higher education and the socioeconomic and cultural homogeneity of the elite participating in it, explain the high degree of institutional homogeneity across universities.

Although the Catholic University emerged as a conservative response to what the Catholic church perceived as the onslaught of liberal, secularizing ideas in the government and the University of Chile (the separation of church and state was formalized only in 1925), the other private universities established during the first half of the twentieth century emerged rather from the desire of regional elites to have their local universities. Thus emerged the University of Concepción (1919), the Federico Santa María Technical University (1926) and the Catholic University of Valparaíso (1928), both in Valparaíso, and the Austral University in Valdivia (1954). The more sparsely populated north of the country saw the creation of its first private university in Antofagasta in 1956. Meanwhile, the Technical State University (now University of Santiago) and the University of Chile extended their reach nationally during the 1950s and 1960s through a network of regional junior colleges.

Such was the makeup of Chilean higher education at the early 1970s: a small and homogeneous system comprising two public universities with presence throughout the country, and six private universities, two of them Catholic, three secular, not-for-profit entities devoted to their region's development, and the last one, the University of the North, with a mixed Catholic-secular status. Such homogeneity of finance, function, and governance was distinctive in Latin America, where public-private distinctiveness has been the norm (Levy, 1986, p. 112). One needs to look outside Latin America, to Belgium and the Netherlands, for example, to find similarly "parallel" (in Geiger's terminology [1986]) public and private sectors.

The military regime of General Augusto Pinochet (1973–1990) fundamentally altered the political economy of Chilean higher education. Public spending in higher education decreased between 15 and 35 percent, depending on the estimate, between 1974 and 1980, forcing the universities to begin charging tuition and to seek other sources of funding. Self-financing in

Chilean universities grew in average from 13 to 27 percent between 1965 and 1980 (Brunner, 1986, pp. 46–47). After introducing sweeping privatizing reforms to labor law, social security, health, capital markets, and education, the military government turned its attention to higher education in the early 1980s. Intent on expanding enrollments, differentiating the higher education system, and bolstering competition, an administrative process was designed for the creation of new private universities and nonuniversity tertiary-level institutions, called professional institutes (offering undergraduate education in applied professional fields), and technical training centers (offering two-year technical and vocational programs). In what many saw as an effort not only to achieve the aforementioned goals but also to reduce and control the potential for political activism of the large public universities, the regional colleges of the University of Chile and the State Technical University were transformed into fourteen small, independent public professional institutes and universities. Public professional institutes were short-lived: they were all gradually upgraded to university status from 1982 to 1994.

A new constitution handed down in 1980 consecrated the "freedom of teaching" as the ideological backbone and juridical cornerstone of education. The concept meant that private individuals were free to receive education from whom they chose and to offer education to whomever would want to take it from them. The role of the state would be to promote the exercise of this freedom and to subsidize private initiatives when they fell short.

In 1990 democracy was reestablished, but the structure of higher education remained unchanged. Thirty years after the privatizing reforms were first introduced, Chile's expenditures in higher education, at 2 percent of gross domestic product (GDP), compare favorably with the Organization for Economic Cooperation and Development's (OECD's) average of 1.4, but 85 percent of that investment comes from private sources, chiefly tuition payments. As a result of the paltry contribution of the public sector to higher education funding, lowest of all OECD countries as a proportion of GDP, tuition levels in Chilean universities rank among the highest in the world as a proportion of GDP per capita, only surpassed according to this measure by U.S. private universities (Organization for Economic Cooperation and Development, 2009, pp. 225–228). The funding structure of Chilean universities reflects this reality: approximately 74 percent of public universities' income comes from tuition payments and research grants, the highest proportion of any country for which comparable data exist (Organization for Economic Cooperation and Development, 2009, p. 230).

Private-Led Growth of Institutions and Enrollments

The institutional platform of higher education expanded and diversified considerably since the liberalizing reforms of 1980. By 1990 there existed sixty universities and 242 nonuniversity postsecondary institutions. Private institutions accounted for practically all of this surge, reaching almost 95 percent of the institutional platform for higher education in 1990 and 78 percent of all universities. The expansion of the public sector from two to sixteen institutions was only apparent, as it was grounded entirely on the elevation to the status of independent universities of the regional branch campuses of the two public universities, while in the "old private" sector the institutional platform has remained unchanged but for three regional campuses of the Catholic University that it spun off in 1992. In other words, only in the private sector did entirely new institutions emerge.

Since 1990 the total number of institutions has decreased by one-third. Again, this reduction is almost solely the result of changes in the private sector and is chiefly to the result of the drastic reduction in the numbers of professional institutes and technical training centers, brought about by regulatory pressure and the failure of small institutions to achieve financial sustainability on the basis of meager tuition income. A similar set of forces brought down the number of private universities from a high mark of forty-five in 1995 to the current thirty-six. The disappearance of a number of private institutions has caused the proportion of the private sector among institutions of higher education to decrease a little, but it still accounts for more than 90 percent of the institutional basis of the system and for almost three-quarters of all universities.

Overall enrollments have expanded sevenfold in the past two decades in the private sector, especially the newly formed institutions, taking up most of this growth. Although public universities increased their student body by

100,000 between 1980 and 2008 (a 236 percent escalation) and old private schools added 74,000 (growing by 272 percent), new private universities, professional institutes, and technical training centers have created 510,000 new openings. In other words, the new private sector is responsible for 74 percent of the surge in enrollments since 1980.

Although in other countries and regions the expansion of private higher education seems to have reached a plateau or is even backing down (Levy, 2009a), in Chile, as in Mexico it continues strong, as the period 2000–2008 shows: the private share of enrollments went from 71 to 78 percent, and private enrollments in universities jumped from 60 to 68 percent. These figures clearly underscore the extent of the private sector's lead in the expansion of tertiary education in Chile.

A generalized driver of the choice of public over private is the fact that in most of the world public institutions charge little or no tuition. It is not the case in Chile. One is led to wonder what would happen to private higher education enrollments globally if this parity of tuition levels across public and private universities were the norm rather than a curiosity.

The Enabling Regulatory Framework

The original licensing mechanism for new institutions of higher education consisted of two phases. First, the legal structure of the new institution had to be administratively approved by the Ministry of Education. Then, for universities and professional institutes, an existing (public or old private) university had to approve the study plans of the proposed programs and agree to examine their students at the end of every term as well as for the final degree exam at the end of the course of studies. Unlike the supervisory arrangements found in other countries, in Chile the new private institution was not affiliated with the examining university. It retained its independence as a legal entity and functioned autonomously, but it could not alter its study programs without the approval of the examining university or pass or graduate its students without the intervention of the examiner.

The procedure proved to be cumbersome. It bogged down the growth of the private sector, which in a decade was not able to reach 20,000 students, contrary to the wishes of the military government. Moreover, it was expensive for the examined institution, which had to pay large fees to the individual examiners and to their university of origin, creating a conflict of interest. Worse, some examining universities had realized that examination fees could become a significant source of income and started taking a larger load than they could reasonably discharge. By the end of the 1980s, five universities were examining a dozen institutions apiece.

Criticism soon emerged about the appropriateness of the examination mechanism to foster growth, allow for diversification of educational projects, and safeguard quality standards. As a result, new legislation was passed in 1990 that completely changed the licensing and supervision requirements. An independent council of higher education, comprised mostly of academics, was created in the structure of the Ministry of Education and charged with the task of supervising private institutions for up to eleven years after their initial opening. If the development of the institution had been satisfactory according to the council, the institution was to be granted full autonomy, which enabled it to offer independently all kinds of degrees anywhere in the country. Unsatisfactory performance would lead to the termination of the authorization of the institution to operate.

From 1990 to 2008, the council closed down fifteen universities and twenty-four professional institutes. A study of the bases for these decisions (Bernasconi and Fernández, 2008) shows that the inability to provide students with the most basic infrastructure, learning resources, and staff faculty was the most common underlying problem. It was, in turn, caused by the failure to enroll students in sufficient numbers. On average, the failed universities had 818 students at the time of their closing (professional institutes were even smaller) and offered just seven study programs on average.

Nowadays, the council oversees only two universities and one professional institute. The rest are fully autonomous institutions (or were closed). Therefore, the institutional base of private higher education can be said to be in a steady state. The same holds for the public sector, with no changes in the institutional makeup since the last remaining public professional institutes were transformed to universities in 1994.

The evolution of the regulatory regime illustrates the theme of "delayed regulation" characteristic of much policymaking around private higher education in the world (Levy, 2005, p. 290) but with a twist. Although in many countries private higher education emerged unregulated or from the interstices of ambiguous legislation, in Chile regulation was clear from the outset, only not, as it turned out, suitable for the trajectory of growth and diversification intended by the government for private higher education. Quality was a concern but not in the sense of alarm at fly-by-night operators' handing out dubious credentials to a gullible or shady clientele. Rather, what was at stake was the quality of the regulatory scheme itself.

Later, quality reemerged as an issue when the newly autonomous private institutions and some public universities began overextending the range and location of their program offerings. An accreditation system was created in 1998 and reinforced in 2006 to deal with the apprehension this situation caused and, more generally, to foster in all institutions a culture of self-assessment and continuous quality improvement.

Accreditation is carried by an autonomous public agency, it is open solely for autonomous institutions, it is not mandatory, and it evaluates, in separate processes, institutions as a whole, undergraduate programs, and graduate programs. After ten years, forty-five of the fifty-seven autonomous universities, eleven of the thirty-one autonomous professional institutes, and eight of the thirty-one autonomous technical training centers obtained accreditation (eight autonomous universities were evaluated and not accredited, and the rest did not apply). Given that it is the smallest institutions that remain outside the accreditation system, institutions that have applied for accreditation represent 96 percent of students enrolled in autonomous institutions of higher education, 99 percent if only universities are considered (Rodríguez, 2009, p. 17).

Private Versus Public: Pluralistic Stratification

Diversification has been a much sought-after but ultimately elusive goal in Chile's higher education policy since the 1980s. The historical basis of the system was highly homogeneous through the early 1970s, at least relative to the rest of Latin America. This circumstance was in part a result of the small number of institutions (Brunner, 1986, p. 24) and, more crucially, to the even distribution of public funding across all institutions. Later, after the reforms of the 1980s, public subsidization was also more or less uniformly withdrawn from public and private institutions alike, forcing both types of institutions to charge tuition and seek out other resources in the market.

The emergence of a new private sector after 1980 increased the diversity of the system in that the new universities were more like undergraduate colleges than complex universities—although research and graduate programs were by then rather undeveloped in the older universities as well. They were also smaller, had no public subsidization or financial aid for their students, and therefore tended to enroll affluent students who could not gain admission in the competitively allocated slots in the other universities. Yet most of the differentiation came from the creation of professional institutes and technical training centers devoted to technical trades and professional occupations not based on academic disciplines.

The dismemberment of the University of Chile and the State Technical University in 1981, however, generated fourteen underfunded, precariously equipped and staffed universities across Chile, many of which have been the object of quality concerns ever since. The same fate awaited the three provincial Catholic universities engendered by the Pontifical Catholic University in 1992 when it decided to rid itself of its regional branch campuses.

What in Chile is called the "traditional" sector of universities therefore comprises the eight original and more consolidated universities and another seventeen newer institutions running the gamut from the up-and-coming, strong, and innovative young universities to the financially struggling, bottom-feeding educational providers of last resort. The only common feature across these twenty-five "traditional" universities is that they are members of Chile's Council of Rectors, a coordinating body for higher education that also serves as a table for negotiation with the Ministry of Education, founded by the original eight in the 1950s and expanded later to include their offspring.

With current enrollment levels, student characteristics no longer differ between the private and the public sectors. With the exception of the Catholic University of Chile, the University of Chile, and a few new private universities catering to the social and economic elite of the country, the student bodies of most institutions are highly diverse. That diversity was reinforced by the introduction in 2005 of a government-backed private loan program to assist poor students in institutions of higher education of all types.

Soft indicators such as news media rankings fail to sustain the hypothesis that strata are directly based on institutional type. "Traditional" universities (public and old privates) are scattered throughout all segments of the rankings but the lowest quintile, while the top ten universities include two publics, three old privates, and five new privates ("Ranking de Universidades 2008," 2008). Selectivity in admissions, measured by the scores of the freshman class in the national academic selection test, shows a similar pattern. In all regional higher education markets in Chile, the most selective institution is an old private, followed closely by a public university, with the exceptions of Santiago and the southern region, where the first place belongs to a public and second to an old private. Only in the Santiago region can new privates be found that are close in selectivity to the most selective traditional universities (Brunner and Uribe, 2007, pp. 278–290). It must be taken into account, however, that competitive conditions between new privates and the rest are not completely neutral, for students in traditional universities enjoy financial aid programs not available to students in new privates.

A recent report by the accreditation agency (Comisión Nacional de Acreditación, 2008) listed the fifteen universities with best results in their institutional accreditation. The list includes the six old privates, five publics, and four new privates. Again, quality is not the exclusive patrimony of one sector or another.

This report does not suggest that Chile's higher education is not stratified by function and prestige. Indeed, indicators of research output and graduate education show that most of the research projects, publications, and doctoral students concentrate in the eight older universities (Organization for Economic Cooperation and Development, 2009, pp. 203–204). Although a handful of new privates are making inroads here as well, it will probably be another five to ten years before we will see one or two new privates interspersed in this group.

Facilitating the development of the private sector in research and doctoral education is thirty years of science policy characterized by project-based allocation of resources. Research funding and scholarships are given with no consideration as to whether it is a private or a public university that supports the petitioner. As the growth of public investment in research outpaces increases in direct institutional subsidy, the private sector is able to tap a growing share of the public resources for higher education.

A rather homogeneous group of public and old private universities is at the apex of the system, comprising the universities with a broader range of functions and missions that include research, technology transfer, and graduate education. Underneath them, the pack is a combination of the rest of the "traditional" set and the new privates, with members of every type occupying spots across the whole spectrum of academic performance. In this sense, Chile's stratification in higher education is pluralistic.

Current Policy Debate

For the better part of the twentieth century, private-public distinctiveness in Chilean higher education was downplayed by nondiscriminatory public funding. Nowadays, the factor diluting observable differences between the two sectors is the opposite: self-financing and deep marketization across the board. Moreover, unlike the typical pattern found in private higher education elsewhere, no discernible mission or function differentiates between the sectors, as old privates have long covered all areas of knowledge and education at both the undergraduate and graduate levels and new privates are increasingly doing the same.

The legitimacy of the private sector, also an issue in private higher education worldwide (see Slantcheva and Levy, 2007, for the case of the former Soviet bloc), is not questioned in Chile. The deep historical roots of private higher education in Chile, the prestige of its most consolidated institutions, both old and new, and its position as the majority sector contribute to its strong social position.

Despite the homogenizing impetus of the funding conditions for higher education in Chile, the lack of functional differentiation, or the legitimacy enjoyed by the private sector, a public-private divide nonetheless exists. As suggested by the evolution of constitutional doctrine mentioned above and the impetus behind each wave of emergence of private institutions in Chile, the respective roles of the state and of private initiative in education have been contentious matters throughout Chile's history (Serrano, 1994, pp. 229–239). The sheer numbers of students in private institutions (and not only at the tertiary level, given that 56 percent of K–12 students are enrolled in private paid or private subsidized schools) keep the matter at the center of the politics of education.

The question of what is and should be the difference between state education and private education is very much in the news in Chile these days. In the case of higher education, the rectors of public universities claim that the government should offer public universities a "new deal," which would free them from administrative regulations hampering their agility, and increase public funding to 50 percent of the universities' budgets. In exchange, the government would get a greater say over the mission, governance, and strategic plans of these universities. Public rectors have also maintained that operational subsidies to private—especially religiously affiliated universities—ought to be revised, as several privates receive larger amounts than most publics.

On the private side, the rectors of five of the six old privates have expressed their frustration with the Council of Rectors as a coordination and policy body, arguing that it contains too varied a set of universities that have in common only the rather accidental fact of their public subsidization. As a manifestation of this situation, they have created a league of universities of their own.

Recent policy reports on Chile's higher education by a blue ribbon presidential commission, the OECD, and the World Bank have delved into the matter of the relationship between the government's universities and the private sector. Recommendations include arguing for a review of the composition and functions of the Council of Rectors in light of the current institutional makeup of Chilean higher education and for a rationalization of funding. This last recommendation presumes new financial arrangements can be based not on the inertia of history but on the contribution of institutions of higher education of every type to the generation of public goods such as research, community outreach, and education for the poor.

Some of this funding philosophy, whereby the state "buys" the public goods it needs from the best provider, regardless of its public or private condition, is very much in accord with the current political economy of the country and has been tried with success both in education and in other sectors (see the Kenyan funding policy debate later). Even if the current policy debate comes to nothing, it is likely that these nondiscriminatory policies will remain, further fostering the development of the private sector as a partner of the state.

Private Higher Education in Bulgaria: Making a Difference

THE EXPANSION OF PRIVATE HIGHER EDUCATION IN BULGARIA is not an isolated phenomenon. After the fall of the communist regimes in 1989, private institutions of higher education multiplied to varying degrees in all countries of Central and Eastern Europe (Slantcheva, 2007b). Although the most cited examples come from Poland, Romania, and Latvia, where almost one-third of all students are enrolled in private institutions, the majority of the Central and Eastern European countries maintain private enrollment patterns ranging between 3 and 20 percent. In academic year 2009–2010, 22 percent of all students in Bulgaria were educated in nine private institutions of higher education (National Statistical Institute, 2010). This private sector evolved gradually over the last nineteen years, establishing itself as distinct from the state sector in terms of funding sources, institutional structures, educational purposes and forms, student base, and social and economic relevance.

The growth of the private provision of higher education across the countries of Central and Eastern Europe, including Bulgaria, is distinguished by several distinctive characteristics. First, the establishment of private institutions in the former communist countries of Europe took place rather quickly (Slantcheva and Levy, 2007). In contrast, private higher education across many neighboring Western European countries played a more "peripheral" role (Geiger, 1986), largely exempted from the global growth scenarios encountered in the rest of the world. Although exceptions to viable private sectors

The primary responsibility for developing this chapter was taken by Snejana Slantcheva-Durst.

exist in Portugal and Spain (Levy, 2009b), small private sectors are still the most common mode and remain largely unacknowledged in the Bologna process—the main vehicle behind the emerging European higher education area and the largest higher education reform effort seen in the world so far (Kwiek, 2007). This omission is thus more relevant to the vibrancy of private sectors in the Central and Eastern European countries that recently joined the European Union. Ten of them, including Bulgaria, became members in 2004 and 2007 and aligned the reform agendas of their higher education systems with the wider processes of Europeanization and harmonization. As some scholars have recognized, however, the apparent disregard for private higher education in European policies thus far has resulted in a failure to offer guidance for country developments and has even thwarted the development of private institutions in countries where external privatization remains one of the very few alternatives for expansion of higher education (Kwiek, 2007, p. 119; Kwiek, 2008).

Second, the appearance of private sectors across Central and Eastern Europe has been rather belated, with only Africa and the Gulf-state regions trailing behind (Slantcheva and Levy, 2007). Very little private provision of higher education existed across the region before the advent of communism. Understandably, the option of using private provision as a reform strategy was not available during the more than forty years of communist rule when higher education was provided solely by centrally controlled state institutions that maintained very low enrollment rates and restricted access. Romania serves as one example of this case, when in 1985 just 10 percent of the age-relevant group was educated in the system (World Bank, 2001).

Last but not least, private higher education in this region should be seen in the context of the larger social, political, and economic transformation of the postcommunist countries where privatization occurred—shifting ownership from the state to private hands—on a massive scale. With respect to higher education, two forms of privatization took place across the region after the fall of the totalitarian regimes: internal and external (Kwiek, 2008, 2009). Internal privatization denotes changes in educational services and ways of operation of state institutions that reflect "reliance on non-governmental revenues, responsiveness to market forces, and incorporation of managerial norms associated with private enterprise" (Johnstone, 2009, p. 6). These internal processes led to a transformation in the mission, aims, organization, management styles, funding patterns, labor relationships, and institutional cultures of public educational institutions (Kwiek, 2009, p. 5). They also meant a change in educational services of these state institutions such as introduction of tuition fees, use of alternative sources of funding, collection of revenues from facilities, outreach services, and engagement in business partnerships. External privatization, on the other hand, refers to the appearance of private institutions alongside existing state institutions. Although both forms of privatization are seen in other countries represented in this volume, the transformations in Central and Eastern Europe were abrupt, simultaneous, and pervasive across the region. In these aspects, the Bulgarian case characterizes the larger regional trends.

The Bulgarian Higher Education System and the Role of Private Higher Education

Three phases characterize the fundamental transformation of the Bulgarian higher education system after the fall of communism in 1989: initial expansion and diversification, subsequent reassertion of state control, and, most recently, alignment with the Bologna framework. During each period of transformation, private institutions have had an active role in introducing innovative approaches and stimulating reform initiatives.

In 1989 the communist regime left behind a higher education system designed to serve a utilitarian society with a centrally planned economy. The system was characterized by tight central control determined by political ideology, low access rates, narrowly specialized programs, preference for certain fields of knowledge and kinds of institutions over others, and historically determined funding mechanisms. The reform of the Bulgarian system of higher education started immediately after the fall of totalitarian rule, occurring "within the framework of an economic crisis of immense dimensions, and teaching staff that, in its majority, were members of the former communist party" (Penkov, 1992, p. 96). A 1990 legislative act restoring academic autonomy served as a catalyst for significant changes in higher education, providing institutions with the long-denied freedoms to define their organizational structure (including the freedom to establish new faculties), academic programs, and courses. The institutions were also given the opportunity to look for additional funding outside the state budget, including the admission of fee-paying students on top of the state-subsidized admissions quota.

As a result, the system of higher education expanded rapidly. This growth of the sector was seen in the large influx of students, many of whom were from nontraditional socioeconomic backgrounds and age groups, and in program and institutional diversity. In five years, student enrollments rose by 40 percent (National Statistical Institute, 2009). In this context, privatization, both external and internal, emerged as the strategy for expansion of the system. New private institutions of higher education appeared and quickly multiplied, bringing with them new practices to the system. Parallel to these developments, new elements were also noted in the state sector of higher education. Most prominently, the numbers of fee-paying students (or students admitted for payment alongside state-subsidized students) at state universities increased dramatically (for example, by 1997 almost half of all students in the state institutions of the country paid tuition fees for their education), and numerous branch campuses of state universities mushroomed throughout the country (Slantcheva, 2007a).

The process of expansion, however, was not accompanied by an increase in state subsidies, internal mechanisms for the regulation of educational quality, or strengthened teaching capacity. Concerns about the diminishing quality of education were especially strong regarding the newly founded institutions and branches, forms of study, and specializations. It was mostly in reaction to the rapidly growing private sector that state-level measures aiming at quality and expansion control were initiated. As a result, the following five years saw the reassertion of state control over higher education. A 1995 law on higher education called for systematic reform and reintroduced practices of centralized micromanagement such as a unified list of programs that institutions were permitted to offer, detailed program requirements, and central determination of institutional budget allocations and student enrollments for all institutions. The National Evaluation and Accreditation Agency was created as a special organ to monitor the level of compliance with these requirements. Four years later, standard tuition fees were introduced, replacing the awkward practice of admitting fee-paying students on top of the state-subsidized quota. In addition, the government initiated a gradual state-induced reduction of student enrollments, defined as the "demassification" of higher education (Popov, 2001) and justified by predictions of a decline in future applicants. In fact, a 2005 report of the World Bank found Bulgaria "unique in its decline in higher education participation" among all members of the European Union (p. iv).

The influence of the Bologna process was felt immediately in the early 2000s. The wider process of European higher education harmonization, exchange, and networking had a positive impact on reform efforts in Bulgaria. The restrictive nature of laws governing the definition of academic courses and programs was loosened, while institutions were given more freedom to determine the number of enrolled students for each specialization. (Nonetheless, state approval of total student enrollments for all institutions, including private ones, remained unchanged.) Quick modifications to the legal framework paralleled efforts to align the educational system with the Europeanwide framework. The diploma supplement and the credit transfer system were introduced as a required component in 2004. These changes also emphasized students' evaluations of faculty, students' participation in university governance systems, development of internal mechanisms for quality control, and regulation of distance learning. Although the system quickly introduced most of the required elements of Bologna, however, much of the change has remained theoretical, with the highest concerns centered on quality assurance and obstacles to mobility. According to the World Bank (2007), "Bulgaria is ranked in the lowest category for participation of students in the quality assurance process, and also scores low on international participation in the quality assessment procedures" (p. 120).

With respect to private provision, a considerable degree of "convergence between the activities undertaken and missions pursued by two sectors in higher education" has taken place in several countries in the region (Pachuashvili, 2008, p. 84), including Bulgaria. The results of this convergence are mixed. On the one hand, state institutions have adopted practices championed in the private sphere such as more businesslike approaches in institutional administration. In this respect, private institutions have introduced effective models of institutional governance and functioning that have been also emulated by decision makers in the public realm. For example, as of 2007 all state institutions in the country are now required by law to introduce external boards of trustees—a feature used only in the private sector up until now. On the other hand, this convergence has had negative implications for private institutions in that the opportunities for the development of private institutions have been sharply narrowed by state-imposed, centralized standards. For example, the distinctive features of the private sector that public institutions are either not willing or not capable to emulate (such as liberal arts education, labor training, short-cycle programs, and strong local focus) are downplayed or even rejected.

In today's Bulgaria, 287,086 students are educated at fifty-three universities and colleges (International Standard Classification of Education [ISCED] levels 5A, 5B, and 6) at the degree levels of professional bachelor (three years), bachelor (four years), master (one to two years), and doctor (National Statistical Institute, 2009). Higher education is still largely organized and financed by the state, with 55.2 percent of its funding coming from public funds, 40 percent from student tuition, 2 percent from other private entities, and 2.8 percent from international sources (Eurydice, 2007, p. 93). The system has achieved much with respect to access (one-third of age-relevant eighteen- to twenty-four-year-olds are enrolled in higher education [Eurydice, 2009]), diversification, harmonization with the European framework, and institutional autonomy. It is one of the European systems with the highest graduation rates (80 percent in ISCED level 5A and 6 and 70 percent in ISCED level 5B), the lowest student-teacher ratios (fewer than fifteen students per teacher), and the lowest levels of teaching expenditures in Europe; it is also one of the countries where the proportion of women graduates of doctoral programs is higher than the average (Eurydice, 2007). At the same time, compared with other countries in the European Union, Bulgaria's tertiary education system is currently characterized by a relatively large number of small and specialized universities, lack of program relevance, inefficient quality assurance mechanisms, and weak accountability of universities (Rauhvargers, Deane, and Pauwels, 2009; World Bank, 2007).

Expansion of Private Higher Education in Bulgaria

Private higher education in Bulgaria does not have a long history. Before communist rule in 1944, the country knew only one private institution of higher education—the Free University of Sofia, established in 1920 and nationalized in 1939 (Boyadjieva, 2003). Private giving for higher establishments was also known—perhaps the largest one being the donation of the brothers Evlogii and Hristo Georgievi, who supported the first institution of higher education in the country, Sofia University. The communist regime eliminated all private provision of education in the country, similar to most communist countries across Central and Eastern Europe.

After the fall of communist rule in the country, private institutions emerged in 1991, signaling the radical transformation of the entire higher education system. They appeared in a legal vacuum; it was not until 1995 that the Bulgarian Parliament officially recognized them. In the matter of just five years, five universities and three colleges were established, educating 10.45 percent of all students in the country. The number of institutions grew to sixteen in 2008–09, or 30.2 percent of all institutions in the country, enrolling 17.5 percent of all students. During this decade of growth, the Bulgarian Parliament closed one private institution of higher education for administrative irregularities—the Slavic University in Sofia (Boyadjieva and Slantcheva, 2007).

Several rationales account for the emergence and growth of the private sector in Bulgaria. According to Weisbrod (1977), a major condition for the private supply of a traditionally public good arises when some social groups express preferences different from the available options offered by a public sector. In this context, Geiger (1985) formulates three major reasons stimulating the appearance of private alternatives to state provision of higher education: "cases in which *more* higher education was demanded than was provided by the state; cases in which groups desired *different* kinds of schools from those provided, and cases in which qualitatively *better* education was sought" (p. 387). All three conditions existed in Bulgaria in 1991. The growing demand for higher education after the fall of the communist regime, stimulated by the sudden liberalization of the former elitist system, outstripped the existing capacity of the state sector. In response, private institutions sprang up to provide education in areas of high demand such as business administration, economics, law, computer sciences, and foreign languages. In this way, private institutions contributed to the expansion of higher education supply, offering more educational opportunities.

New and different organizational forms were also pioneered in the private sector such as the departmental structure and bachelor and master degrees, and alternative educational approaches were tested, including distance learning and modular course arrangements. Further, liberal arts education was introduced, credit systems were developed, and standardized tests were implemented. Foreign partnerships in creating institutions and offering services were also introduced in those early years. Finally, in these early years of transition, two private institutions appeared with the explicit mission to offer education better than the existing provision. The New Bulgarian University and the American University in Bulgaria promised to lead to the creation of a new, alternative, more dynamic, and free educational system of higher education. Both institutions aimed to train the future leaders of the country and the region and to lead the way to future social transformation.

Private institutions do not always share common characteristics, and different authors have used a variety of criteria to capture their nature (Altbach, Reisberg, and Rumbley, 2009; Levy, 1986; Reisz, 2003). Purpose, ownership, funding sources, control by government, operation, and management styles have been most often discussed as useful measures of private systems. In the Bulgarian context, private institutions of higher education are nonprofit by law, founded by given individuals or organizations, governed by external boards and senior professional administration, and reliant on tuition fees as a major revenue source. At the same time through the legislative framework, the state exercises strong external control over the private sector. In fact, private institutions in Bulgaria are often labeled government-dependent private institutions (Eurydice, 2007, 2009).

In the private higher education literature, different typologies have been developed to capture the variance in institutional character from both global (Geiger, 1986; Levy, 1986, 2005, 2008b) and Central and Eastern European perspectives (Reisz, 2003). A typology useful for the Bulgarian case separates existing kinds of private institutions into three main types based on their roles, motives, ownership, and management (Levy, 2008b, 2009b; Praphamontripong, 2008a). Those three types group private institutions into elite or semi-elite, religious or cultural, and nonelite or demand absorbing. In addition, some category cross-cutting considerations are given to for-profit institutions and private-public partnerships (Levy, 2009b).

The majority of private institutions in Bulgaria fall mostly under the demand-absorbing type. Private provision is rather uneven in Bulgaria, and of all private institutions, three are among the top ten of all institutions in the country by size, while all others, except one, have fewer than one thousand students (World Bank, 2007). Most of these institutions are "concentrated in institutions not labeled university" (Levy, 2009b, p. 18). They are smaller, focus mostly on teaching, and have a relatively narrow programmatic scope of occupationally oriented programs, concentrating on management, marketing, economics, agricultural studies, insurance and finances, tourism, computer sciences, and theater. They are primarily student oriented, often closely connected with the labor market, and regionally engaged. An interesting development in the Bulgarian context, found also in several other Central and Eastern European countries (and discussed in the chapters on Mexico and Thailand in this volume), is the consistent growth over the past decade of institutions of the professional, short-cycle college type, offering shorter, occupationally oriented programs and qualifications at the ISCED 5B level. In fact, it is in this sector that private higher education in Bulgaria marks its largest growth in both institutions and student enrollments (Table 2). These institutions have managed to successfully adapt to shifting labor markets, respond to growing demand for training in market-relevant fields, and address regional needs. Contrary to developments in other countries in the region (Pachuashvili, 2008), demand for private universities in Bulgaria remains high and is still growing; by contrast, demand for public universities in the country is leveling off (World Bank, 2007).

A small number of the private universities and specialized schools can also be successfully classified as semielite institutions. An interesting development in the Bulgarian context, noted as well by Praphamontripong (2008a) in the framework of Thai higher education (see also "Public Policy and the Growth

TABLE 2
Bulgarian State and Private Institutions of Higher Education, by Type of Institution and Student Enrollments

	Academic Year 1999–2000	Academic Year 2008–2009	Percent Change
All Colleges and Universities			
Higher Education Institutions	46	53	15.22
Higher Education Enrollments	261,321	274,247	4.95
State Colleges (ISCED 5B) and Universities (ISCED 5A and 6)			
State-Regulated Independent Colleges (ISCED 5B)	2	1	−50.0
Colleges at State Universities (ISCED 5B)	38	28	−26.3
Students in State Colleges (ISCED 5B)	15,945	8,451	−47.0
Universities (ISCED 5A and 6)	37	36	−2.7
Students in State Universities (ISCED 5A and 6)	242,860 (including 3,091 doctoral)	207,416 (including 3,949 doctoral)	−14.59
Private Colleges (ISCED 5B) and Universities (ISCED 5A and 6)			
Independent Colleges (ISCED 5B)	2	9	350
Colleges at State Universities (ISCED 5B)	4	0	−100
Students in Private Colleges (ISCED 5B)	2,516	19,273	666
Universities (ISCED 5A and 6)	5	7	40
Students in Private Universities (ISCED 5A and 6)	24,898 (no doctoral)	39,052 (including 55 doctoral)	57

Source: National Statistical Institute, 2010.

of Private Higher Education in Thailand" in this volume), is that those private institutions that appeared first and were first granted recognition are considered the elites of the private sector—or the "semielites." In Bulgaria's case, four universities and specialized schools have gained prominence both regionally and nationally, offering good practical teaching and training and some applied research (Levy, 2009b). Some of them exhibit successful partnerships with foreign institutions. In general, foreign partnerships are a strong feature of the private sector at both universities and colleges, offering foreign recognized degrees and foreign accreditation. Yet foreign accreditation is not recognized in the Bulgarian legislative context, which presents a challenge to those institutions. No private institution of the religious/cultural type has emerged yet. In fact, the only officially recognized religious college in the country, the College for Islamic Studies, exists as a publicly funded, independent vocational institution.

Public Policy Surrounding Private Higher Education

The Bulgarian system of higher education is strongly regulated by its legislative framework. Similar to the situation in many postcommunist countries in Central and Eastern Europe, fitting private colleges and universities in the national higher education policy framework has occurred in waves. Public policy toward private higher education has been mostly reactive, often recognizing already established developments in the private sector or curtailing trends deemed inappropriate.

Since their inception, private institutions have been one step ahead of public policy. The official grant of recognition to private institutions as legitimate members of the higher education community occurred only after degrees were already being awarded. It is no doubt true that legal grounds permitting nongovernmental provision of higher education were already given with the 1990 Law on Academic Autonomy immediately after the fall of the communist regime. Nevertheless, a legal vacuum in terms of quality requirements, structural arrangements, or operational details accompanied the first years of functioning of the Bulgarian private sector. It was not until 1995 that private institutions of higher education were actually registered as entities in the legal framework of Bulgarian higher education policy. Subsequent changes and amendments of the higher education law gradually recognized one or another alternative aspect of their governance, functioning, and educational processes, most often after the respective aspect has been long in place—an issue of "delayed regulation" (Levy, 2005) also discussed in the chapter on Chile in this volume. The academic community of traditional state universities has had strong influence in directing public policy through close involvement in advisory committees, influential academic figures, or the Council of Rectors.

The reactive process of fitting private institutions in a still rather rigid national legal framework catering to state institutions does not reflect a state policy that promotes difference but one that is attempting to standardize the provision of higher education. The greatest challenge to the private sector in Bulgaria, and to the system in general, remains the lack of opportunities to recognize and capitalize on differences exhibited by these relatively new institutions. Several paradoxes continue to accompany the development of the private sector as a result of this approach.

The first concerns accreditation, which in the Bulgarian context (similar to the Kenyan case) means compliance with state-imposed standards and norms. In their attempts to receive institutional and program accreditation, private institutions of higher education have to follow state standards that accommodate the practices of older and larger state universities. Thus, in effect accreditation standards are reinforcing "a kind of transfer of the image of public institutions onto private institutions" (Kolasiński, Kulig, and Lisiecki, 2003, p. 438). As a consequence, institutions that have a distinctively different character such as liberal arts universities or short-cycle labor-market-aligned colleges—kinds of institutions seen mostly in the private sector face the constant challenge of balancing their specific character with centrally imposed criteria to which they are often not suited.

The reinforcement of the image of public institutions onto private institutions is further compounded by additional factors such as the "negative stereotypes" inherited from the past and still holding private provision as "something worse" and the heavy reliance of private institutions on part-time lecturers from public institutions (Kolasiński, Kulig, and Lisiecki, 2003,

p. 438). The high number of part-time faculty hired from state universities (who also hold full-time jobs at public universities) is a concern shared by both the decision makers and the academic community. In academic 2009–2010, 61 percent of all faculty employed in the private sector were on part-time basis, compared with 36 percent in the public sector (National Statistical Institute, 2010).

Another paradox concerns the centralized determination of student enrollments for both the state and private sectors. Private institutions are not subsidized by the public purse; at the same time, their enrollments and indirectly institutional revenue are capped by the state. This challenge remains as an old, unsettled issue despite the determined lobbying efforts of the private sector.

Finally, admission patterns are yet another issue with a rather long history. Lower access requirements are more common to private institutions in general; those institutions often serve as a second port of entry into the system to students unable to pass successfully entrance examinations to state institutions. Unfortunately, although the public debate raises the concern of those students' low academic preparation, there has been little acknowledgment of the positive role of those institutions in expanding educational opportunities or any discussion of these institutions' increased need for support required for adequate preparation of a more challenging student body. A most recent gain for the private, nonuniversity institutions has been the "upgrading" of the three-year degree of "specialist" to the degree of professional bachelor (a brand-new degree for the system). This development was not met with enthusiasm by the state sector, which openly opposed it through the Council of Rectors (Radev, 2009).

Conclusion

Private institutions in Bulgaria have managed to preserve and strengthen a distinctive character known for their accessibility, responsiveness to the labor market, alternative educational approaches, and strong regional involvement. Throughout their evolution, Bulgarian private institutions have often had to deal with a rigid legal framework and negative public perceptions. Usually judged in comparison with their public counterparts, private institutions have often been blamed for low academic standards, a weak research base, open admissions, and nonstandard practices. Coupled with these factors have also been the negative attitudes toward professional short-cycle institutions. The achievements of the private institutions have gradually brought them increased legal and social recognition. According to a 2007 study of the social legitimacy of the private sector in Bulgaria, the private institutions appear to lag behind state institutions in legitimacy and remain more invisible compared with their state counterparts (Boyadjieva and Slantcheva, 2007). Increasingly, however, a significant part of the Bulgarian population is demonstrating an openness to consider their advantages and to recognize the opportunities they offer.

Growth in Kenyan Private Higher Education

THIS CHAPTER ANALYZES KENYAN private higher education from the perspective of its role in the expansion of higher education and the current policy environment and debates on the place of private higher education in higher education generally. A limitation rarely avoidable in discussions on private higher education in Africa is the concentration of such discussions on universities to the neglect of nonuniversity private higher education. The glorification of university education is largely to blame for this preoccupation, as the inherent belief is in the power of a degree as opposed to a diploma. Indeed, in Kenya some practitioners have lamented the "demise" of middle-level colleges (Nyaigoti-Chacha, 2004). The situation is not helped by the lack of data on nonuniversity private higher education that makes a secondary analytical work like the current one an arduous task. With this limitation noted, the chapter therefore concentrates on private universities.

Background

The African experience in private higher education strongly echoes global historical and contemporary patterns, regardless of the prism of analysis one adopts: from the causes of growth, forms of growth, types of institutions, finance, governance, status, and roles (Levy, 2007d). Its arrival is therefore both "conventional" and "unremarkable"—which is not to say that nothing is special in African private higher education in terms of its role or innovation: it is only that it conforms to a generally known pattern. Although this observation

The primary responsibility for developing this chapter was taken by Wycliffe Otieno.

is mostly true, the template may not apply uniformly across the continent, given its diversity. In some systems, the emergence was for completely different reasons. Kruss's analyses (2002, 2007) show that in South Africa, the excess demand does not explain the emergence and growth of private higher education. Rather, it is the demand for "better" or "different" education intertwined with a demand for "more" education.

Nevertheless, it is broadly true that the emerging prominence that private higher education commands in Africa is a direct consequence of the excess demand for higher education and the inability of the public system to meet that demand (Ajayi, Goma, and Johnson, 1996). This "public failure"—the inability of the public institutions to enroll a sufficient number of the eligible age group—that currently stands at about 4 percent and a gradual erosion of capacities of governments to continue high subsidies for public universities provided the initial impetus to private growth. In the midst of this failure, the government tacitly endorsed the important role private providers play in expanding access to higher education.

The close link between the emergence (and "surge") in private higher education and the fall of the iron curtain in Africa must not be missed. The fall of communism saw the end of protectionist aid that most African governments had enjoyed for a long time. Starved of cash, public institutions faced severe cuts in their budgets. With the endorsement of post–World War II international monetary organizations, the governments began embracing neoliberal economic policies that entailed opening up their markets, allowing greater private sector participation, and divesting from enterprise control. Policies were designed to legitimize this shift. For Africa, the World Bank published two influential reports (World Bank, 1985), and African countries used these documents as the basis for domesticating proprivate investment policies. Kenya, for example, published—hot on the heels of the World Bank publication—a macroeconomic chapter called *Economic Management for Renewed Growth* in 1986 (Kenya National Assembly, 1986) and followed it two years later with a sessional paper, *Education and Manpower Training for the Next Decade and Beyond* (Kamunge, 1988). In the sessional paper, the government officially endorsed privatization of education, which followed the enactment of new legislation for regulating private higher education.

The new law was called the Universities Act, Chapter 210B of the Laws of Kenya. It provided for the establishment of the Council on Higher Education with nineteen functions, including promoting the objectives of university education; accrediting universities; ensuring the maintenance of standards; advising the government on the standardization, recognition, and equation of degrees, diplomas, and certificates; and arranging for registration, visitations, and inspection of private universities, among others. Four years later, in 1989, a subsidiary regulation, Legal Notice No. 56 (The Universities [Establishment of Universities] Standardization, Accreditation, and Supervision Rules, 1989) was put in place to control private higher education (Abagi, Nzomo, and Otieno, 2005).

The law spells out clear guidelines for accreditation of institutions. It is a two-stage process beginning with the granting of a Letter of Interim Authority, a license allowing an institution to operate. Institutions that existed before the law came into effect fall in the second category of "registered" universities. Once the institutions fulfill all requirements for a private university, they are granted charters—the full and final accreditation. Only institutions in these categories are authorized to advertise and mount approved degree programs.

The role of the commission has come into sharp focus because of its stringent policing of private universities as opposed to public ones. This role has had its benefits, specifically in ensuring that these institutions conform to high requirements of quality. Indeed, quality is a difficult concept to measure, but proxies such as low lecturer-student ratios, better facilities, and motivated staff are more evident in private universities, even if not uniformly. The commission is empowered to reinspect private institutions any time it deems fit or suspects that quality is compromised. To a great extent, this power has served as a check on private growth. Instead of expanding, private institutions spend significant resources maintaining standards.

Establishment and Growth of Private Universities

All major works on private universities in Kenya have documented their religious origins and domination. A number of institutions existed before independence as missionary colleges, while some were established after independence but before the enactment of appropriate statutes to regulate their operations. Leading among them are the United States International University (USIU), the largest and the most secular university; University of Eastern Africa at Baraton (UEAB); Daystar University; and Catholic University of Eastern Africa (CUEA). Apart from USIU, all major private universities remain religious. Between them, they account for slightly more than 20,000 students.

The extent to which the Kenyan case typifies Levy's well-presented private surge (1986) is arguable. It has been a gradual, less intense, regulated growth but one that remains relatively small by enrollment standards. The number of institutions has increased substantially following the enactment of relevant statutes to regulate private higher education, but compared with the public universities, the pace of enrollment in private universities has been slow. The Kenyan case is therefore one of a public surge, a surge that is itself a product of privatization. The extent to which this private-driven public surge was anticipated—in fact, any anticipation of partial public privatization and its impact on the growth of private higher education—is debatable. A fact not disputed is that it has significantly slowed down private growth.

The sharpest enrollment increase was in the public sector's privately sponsored Module II program (that is, enrolling nongovernment-supported students), which more than tripled between 2000 and 2007. This sharp increase in public enrollment explains the slow private growth. Otieno's estimation (2002) of total private share of university enrollment by 2002 was 20 percent, but by 2006, it had shrunk to 18.6 percent, thanks to the privately run programs introduced by the public universities from the late 1990s. These programs have become so popular that in the large public universities like the University of Nairobi and Kenyatta University, they constituted more than 50 percent of total enrollment in 2008–2009 and accounted for the bulk of institutional revenue, sometimes more than public funding. Given the tradition, public financing privilege, wide array of popular programs, and best faculty, among others, checks on private growth were perhaps a foregone conclusion. The critical questions are how private institutions survive and the strategies they employ to retain their market share.

Four institutions that are accredited under the "registered" system are those that were granted the registration in 1989 when the private higher education statute was enacted. They have more or less remained in the same category. In addition to the pressure from a privatizing public, the limited growth in enrollment at private universities is partly to be blamed on the reluctance of some institutions in this category to expand their programs beyond the mainstream religious curriculum on which they were founded. Although some newer universities have succeeded in diversifying the curriculum, most of the older ones have not expanded their capacity sufficiently.

Overall, capacity in the private universities has increased by only a few hundred over time in sharp contrast to the public universities (Mwiria and others, 2007). An emerging dynamic is the extent to which some of the new enterprising and secular institutions add both to the competition among private universities and with the public sector. Some new private universities like Mt. Kenya University have started with huge capacities and pose a challenge—and set the trend—for the older private ones. Pioneers such as USIU, Daystar University, and CUEA have remained the largest institutions in terms of enrollment.

These universities have established a reputation in private university education, and their courses are in demand. The USIU has had to put applicants on waiting lists because of limited space (Mwiria and Ng'ethe, 2002). How long this dominance will be retained is one of the interesting aspects of private higher education in Kenya to watch in the years to come.

Private Provision and Positive Change?

The debate on the role of private higher education has evolved. It is no longer about necessity, nor even relevance, but about substantive issues of equity in the application of regulatory laws, funding, and, fundamentally, quality. Kenya has debated these issues for a long time. Though not informed by it, the debate clearly echoes the questions raised by Mabizela (2003) and Kruss (2007) in their analyses of the difference that private providers are making in higher education. Whereas the central thesis of Kruss's postulates is the private claim to offer better, quality education as opposed to the public, Mabizela concentrates on the enormity of challenges facing these institutions and the need to address these challenges if they are to remain relevant. The shift must entail a focus away from the current preoccupation with profiteering to improved quality. The claim to better quality can be realized only by investing in "quality enhancers."

The Quality Imperative

Mabizela (2003) contends that even in areas where private higher education institutions identify and concentrate on particular niches, it is not a given that they will excel in them and that, in fact, evidence points to low-quality offerings. He cites the South African example where an investigation by the Council on Higher Education (CHE) in 2003 found institutions do not always offer the necessary knowledge, skills, and competencies needed by young higher education graduates. The Kenyan experience proves otherwise. The leading private university, USIU, for example, has striven to offer business programs and MBA programs that are the most sought-after academic credentials. Only the costs bar most would-be applicants. Daystar University has also excelled in communications, while the UEAB has made a mark in nursing degrees. On education, the CUEA has turned out to be a serious competitor to public universities. These features attest to a serious private sector striving to offer the best. Two factors have made it possible. First is the stringent regulation by the CHE, which requires very high standards that some private universities have argued are unreasonable. But the CHE seems to have played its role of watchdog well. Institutions that have had run-ins with the regulator are ironically not local, but foreign Western universities. A second reason for private seriousness is the competition from the rapidly privatizing public that forces the private universities to work extra hard to counter the public onslaught. This situation affects mostly new entrants, as the older ones have established traditions.

Whether the standards set in Kenya compare with the rest of the world is debatable. Bernasconi's exposition (2003) of the genuine drive by Chilean universities to offer real, quality academic programs that even challenge the public appear to be a rare superior standard but one that a few Kenyan private universities can rightfully claim to strive for. Whether they equal it is another matter altogether. What the Kenyan case clearly shows is that those institutions that attempt to offer low-quality education die a natural death, as students shun them. One such case can be cited in the Kiriri Women's University of Science and Technology (KWUST) that was set up as the first women-only university in East and Central Africa. The KWUST has found it hard to thrive in an environment where competitors have cut niches in specific fields. The KWUST's experience is an irony because it is one of the few secular private universities in Kenya. The KWUST case is not so much a failure in meeting standards but in that it chose to innovate in an area not tested before and found difficulty in accessing a sufficient pool of female students to make a whole university viable. Competition with the public sector is relevant here too, as public universities have expanded their capacities substantially to enroll more students in revenue-generating programs such as science and technology. As evidence of the public-private competition, it is clear that private universities do not have an upper hand in these programs.

The Regulatory Framework

Debate on regulation of private higher education has revolved around the mandate of the CHE. Although it was set up and given nineteen statutory functions, Nyaigoti-Chacha (2004) laments the commission's preoccupation with the accreditation of private universities. It is accused of making the playing field uneven to the advantage of public universities and using a public university standard in certifying private university programs. Although public universities remain autonomous because they are set up by independent acts of parliament, the private universities are required to adhere to very stringent requirements that do not apply to the public counterparts. The government has tried to sort out the problem by establishing a committee to work on a harmonized legal instrument for the entire education sector. The outcome is a bill that proposes to abolish these independent acts and bring all universities under one law. The bill is yet to be taken to Parliament, but public universities are vigorously campaigning to ensure it is not enacted.

Elite Versus Nonelite Private Higher Education

The debate on the quality or otherwise of private institutions should be anchored on the dichotomy of elite versus nonelite institutions as expounded by Levy (1986). By its very nature, virtually all private universities in Kenya could be classified as elite—not in terms of academic content or quality but in the very fact that their expensive nature locks out a certain segment of the population. Indeed, a fourth factor in the slow pace of increase in enrollment in these institutions (besides lack of a diverse curriculum, privatizing public universities, and intraprivate university competition) is their elitism. Although all private universities are expensive, the USIU stands in a league of its own and is arguably the most elitist institution in the country. Its fees are sometimes double the fees in some private universities. Surprisingly, this intraprivate university cost differential is one of the least debated aspects of private higher education in Kenya. In the highly capitalist and liberal market that Kenya is, the lack of engagement is not altogether confounding.

The Religious Foundation of a Secularizing Private Higher Education and Curriculum

This area is another one in which private higher education is trying to reengineer itself. It should be noted that although the law was put in place around 1985, the first institutions to take advantage of it were religious. Not only had they existed before most secular institutions but also the religious institutions wielded a power and influence over the state that helped their applications be processed much more quickly. Although the USIU had existed from 1969, the first university to be granted a charter was the Seventh Day Adventist UEAB. The second was the Pentecostal Daystar, and the third was the Catholic CUEA. Even the little-known Scott Theological College was chartered ahead of the prestigious USIU. This trend continued so that even the secular universities that had religious affiliation or ownership such as the Aga Khan University in Esmailia preceded most truly secular institutions. The other secular universities that gained faster accreditation owe it to their political connections. It might be expected that their political nature would affect the quality of these institutions. Surprisingly, it is not the case. Although a political connection might speed the license, it would not guarantee the flow of students. On this particular front, Kenyan institutions find that they just have to deliver.

The Challenge of a Diverse Curriculum

The next religious attribute, apart from ownership, is curriculum. In the initial years, a majority were satisfied with a largely religious content. Virtually all chartered private universities had theological courses but not many science and technology disciplines. The trend is changing, as more religious institutions are rapidly secularizing their curricula. It is not that the religious courses are being abandoned but that the institutions are diversifying to remain competitive. Secularization applies only to curriculum, not to ownership, and Otieno (2002) suggests Kenya's religious university communities offer apparently opposing pursuits. Religious owners seem to want to penetrate and optimize the benefits of the market (that is, maximize monetary gains) and not to evangelize at any cost (Otieno, 2002). Things have changed rapidly, and religious universities no longer try to hide their profit motive.

The success with which even the religious universities have been able to reform their curricula to attract more students, however, remains limited. Mwiria and others' detailed examination (2007) of the curriculum offered in private universities does not show much diversity. It is neither scientific nor technological and almost predictably includes business studies. Only about 1 percent of all students in private universities are enrolled in fields classified as scientific or technological. This situation has led to the criticism that although more females are enrolled in these institutions (at an average of 51 percent of all enrollments), the institutions continue to channel females in the traditional, supposedly feminine fields. Contrary to the position taken by Onsongo (2007), the institutions have not therefore provided the breakthrough that females require to compete with males favorably in certain professions. The reason for this discrepancy is both difficult to understand and rarely debated and studied. Whereas medicine is one of the most competitive courses locally, it is so far offered by only one private and two public universities; moreover, the CUEA has one of the best and biggest hospitals in the capital city but has never considered operating a school of medicine, although it certainly has the resources and personnel to administer a medical program. The slow development of new curricula suggests the pace of curriculum reforms in private universities is often out of sync with market trends.

The tough competitive environment in which private universities operate ought to have naturally forced them to diversify to survive. The pace set by the newly established Madurai Kamaraj University is sending ripples across public and other established private universities and appears to stimulate new competition. Indeed, a notable positive feature of the private evolution is the challenge some enterprising, innovative institutions pose both to mainstream public universities and smaller private universities.

Financing

Public funding for private education has not attracted much attention, partly because it is not expected. Levy notes that especially in the developing world, "a key baseline is that public funding of private higher education is the exception, not the rule" (2007c, p. 49)—which is true even for much of the developed world. In Kenya, lack of government support for private institutions is one of the current issues of debate. The argument is twofold. First, these institutions complement the role of the publicly funded ones in providing space for students left out of an ineffective public selection system. Second, the system has no private students per se, as public institutions are funded by public taxes to which parents of students in private institutions also contribute. This debate is far from settled in Kenya, but the higher education loans board has now extended its loans to students in private universities.

The most recent figures for loan disbursement by university type are unavailable, but data from 2002–2003 (Otieno, 2004) attest to attempts made by the government to indirectly fund private universities. The ratio of private to public university loan recipients was more than 1:3, much higher than the overall enrollment ratio of about 1:5. The difference is stark, however, when the proportion of total tuition fees covered by loans for private and public university students is considered. The average cost of private university fees is eight to ten times that of the public, subsidized stream (Otieno, 2003).

It is also evident that only a few university students apply for the publicly funded loans, which could be the result of two factors. First is the socioeconomic profile of the students. Most come from the upper-income groups where debt is uncommon and perhaps also socially unwelcome. Second is a general perception that the loans are earmarked for public university students. Otieno (2004) points out that if this category of students is eliminated together with the 22 percent enrolled in parallel programs, only about half the students in universities apply for loans. It would therefore not be farfetched to argue that those who do not receive loans constitute less than 20 percent of the entire university population.

The public budget also supports staff salaries, food and accommodation allowances, tuition fees in public universities, and basic infrastructure funded by the government's development budget. Salaries and infrastructure constitute the heaviest expenditures, support the public cannot afford for private universities.

Conclusion

The path that private universities in Kenya have trudged is a long one. They have evolved from being an alternative to the public provision of education to existing in an environment where survival is the first priority. The competition from the public sector creates a difficult situation that challenges typical narratives of the advantages of private higher education in countries with more demand-absorbing scenarios. An understanding of private growth is incomplete in the absence of the public pressure. It is easy to argue that many of the reasons for failure to compete effectively rest with the private universities. An analysis of state policies and practice, however, could improve our understanding. Such argument misses the point on how restrictive some policies or practice could be to the growth of private higher education. It might be necessary to reform the policies or regulatory frameworks to allow private players to operate on an equal footing. In Kenya, for example, the law requires private universities to have a minimum of fifty acres of land before it can be granted a charter, even if it has met all other requirements. For a technologically driven university or one that specializes in information technology and business studies, such a requirement is plainly ridiculous because it does not add value to the core function of the institution. Other policies that might require review relate to private access to public resources. For example, loans constitute a big proportion of the income of public universities, and the extension of the loans to private university students was controversial. Once loans to private higher education students were allowed, the debate moved to a second level on the equity and effectiveness of the current loan allocation levels in public versus private universities.

Both the new and old private higher education institutions attest to some positive developments in Kenyan private higher education. Yet it is not that these institutions have brought about tremendously new innovation. It is rather that they have overcome the initial skepticism on their viability, quality, and relevance in a turf long dominated by privileged public universities. That they have not taken over and led in enrollments is not so much because of their noncompetitiveness but because of the enduring tradition of public privilege. The ongoing partial public privatization in Kenya is attributed to the private challenge to public domination that required an effective public counterresponse. From the enrollment figures, the public sector seems to have taken the initial advantage away from the private sector. Ironically, private universities may therefore have inadvertently helped public universities in Kenya entrench their dominance.

Private Higher Education in Dubai: Growing Local Versus Importing Foreign Campuses

ONLY RECENTLY HAS PRIVATE HIGHER EDUCATION DEVEL-OPED a significant foothold in many Arab nations. Indeed, even though some places throughout the region such as Baghdad, Cairo, and Beirut are cities of ancient learning, development of the tertiary education system in much of the gulf region (Bahrain, Kuwait, Oman, Qatar, Saudi Arabia, and the United Arab Emirates [UAE]) has been limited to the last few decades and largely in the public sector. Private higher education is now growing, however, and much of its expansion has occurred because of relatively distinctive government policies, fostering some innovative organizational developments (see, for example, Croom, 2010, and Lane, 2010a).

Regionally, private higher education first developed largely to provide an American-style higher education experience that was different from what was otherwise available (if educational access existed at all). For example, the American University of Beirut, a private, nonsectarian institution, was founded in 1866 in Lebanon. Similar private, nonprofit "American" universities have been established in Egypt (1919), Kuwait (2004), Iraq (2007), and the United Arab Emirates. Access to private higher education remained very limited for much of the twentieth century, however. In the last decade, though, private higher education in many nations in the Middle East has grown significantly, "regardless of regime type, whether harshly authoritarian or semi-democratic, whether pro- or anti-Western" (Levy, 2006, p. 26).

The primary responsibility for developing this chapter was taken by Jason F. Lane.

A significant challenge to understanding the higher education sectors in this region can be the very blurred line that separates public and private higher education. In part, the difficulty in discerning the distinction is the result of changing and relatively specific relationships between institutions and the local government. Government control can shift (and some have absolute power); thus, private institutions may become nationalized or national institutions may turn private. Moreover, part of the growth of higher education now includes partnerships with and investment by foreign educational institutions. In addition to the growing domestic private higher education sector, several international branch campuses (IBCs) have been established in the Middle East, including in Bahrain, Jordan, Qatar, and the United Arab Emirates (Becker, 2009; Verbik and Merkley, 2006). In some cases, special "free zones" have been created to exempt IBCs from local regulations, and some governments (or their agents) have provided significant financial incentives to offset the monetary costs of a university to establish and operate a branch campus (see Lane, forthcoming; Verbik and Merkley, 2006). The Dubai International Academic City and Qatar's Education City exempt institutions from many local laws, and Abu Dhabi and Qatar provided such resources as new buildings and operating capital; thus, even though the government does not have direct control over the IBCs, the level of support provided raises questions about where to classify these institutions along the private-public continuum.

This chapter explores the development of public, private, and free-zone institutions in the UAE, with a specific focus on Dubai, which is the emirate that has had the fastest-growing private higher education sector. Although the public sector has developed largely as part of federal planning, growth of the private sector has been the result of policy choices in each emirate. Further, a critical lack of study of or documented knowledge about the development of higher education in the various emirates is apparent. This chapter draws on coauthor Lane's field work in Dubai, including interviews with academic leaders and policymakers and analysis of documents and data from government agencies, media outlets, and nongovernmental organizations.

Development of Public Higher Education in the United Arab Emirates

More than one hundred years after the founding of the American University in Beirut, the land that is now the United Arab Emirates was largely without any sort of infrastructure such as roads, hospitals, or schools (Abdullah, 1978; Swaroop, 2004). The nation, founded in 1971, emerged from a federation of Bedouin tribes that were first grouped together in the 1800s as Trucial Sheikhdoms, eventually coming under British protection in 1892. The seven emirates that now make up the UAE continue to operate as a federation. Although Abu Dhabi serves as the nation's capital, each emirate retains extensive (although not absolute) control over its internal affairs. Indeed, education is one of the policy arenas in which both the federal and emirate governments seek regulatory dominance. As such, the regulatory and policy environments remain very much in flux, and the resulting tensions have affected the development of the private higher education sector.

In almost four decades, the country has grown significantly from a population of about 250,000 people who had access to only seventy-four primary schools and no domestic form of postsecondary education (Abdullah, 1978; Swaroop, 2004). As of 2009, the population of the UAE reached 6 million people, fewer than 20 percent of whom were UAE citizens (Department of Economic and Social Affairs, Population Division, 2009). Thirty percent of the national population (1.77 million) reside in Dubai (Dubai Statistics Center, 2010). Moreover, the nation's postsecondary higher education sector now includes three public federal institutions and an additional sixty-four institutions licensed by the federal Ministry of Higher Education and Scientific Research, not including dozens of institutions operating in free zones exempted from federal regulation (Commission on Academic Accreditation, 2010; Knowledge and Human Development Authority, 2010; Lane, 2010a).

At the federal level, the higher education system falls under the purview of the Ministry of Higher Education and Scientific Research. Three federal institutions (the United Arab Emirates University, Higher Colleges of Technology, and Zayed University) make up the national public higher education sector and, with very few exceptions, are open only to UAE nationals, whose education is paid for by the government. The oldest institution, United Arab Emirates University, was founded in 1976 and is located in the city of Al-Ain, in the emirate of Abu Dhabi.

During the 1980s, in an effort to stem the increasing number of students studying abroad and address fears of a brain drain, the national government formed the higher colleges of technology (HCT) to provide nationals with additional access to applied, technically oriented diplomas and bachelor-level degree programs in business, education, engineering technology, information technology, communications technology, and health sciences. Over the next several years, the HCTs evolved into a fourteen-campus system located throughout the nation and educating the largest number of UAE citizens each year; enrollments now exceed 16,000 (HCT Factbook, 2009).

In response to the increasing number of female students desiring to pursue a postsecondary degree, the federal government in 1998 created the third federal institution: Zayed University (now with campuses in Abu Dhabi and Dubai). Although the institution originally enrolled only women, the Zayed campuses now provide bachelor's and master's programs for more than 3,000 female and male students, most of whom continue to be female (Zayed University, 2009). Courses continue to be segregated, with women and men attending classes at different times. Of particular note, enrollments in all three federal institutions are dominated by female students. At the HCTs, which have separate campuses for women and men, enrollments at the women's colleges exceed those of their male counterparts. A similar situation is seen in the UAE University, where female students accounted for almost 78 percent of the 12,865 students enrolled in 2007–2008 (United Arab Emirates University, 2008). In fact, when the UAEU launched the first Ph.D. program offered by a federal institution in January 2010, twenty-eight of the thirty-eight students were women (Swan, 2010).

Private Higher Education in Dubai: Institutional and Programmatic Overview

The private higher education sector in Dubai now comprises a complex collection of institutions. Some are grown locally; some are imported from other nations. Some are for profit; some are nonprofit. Some are licensed and accredited by the federal government; others are licensed by the Dubai government but not accredited locally. Some institutions offer a full comprehensive curriculum, others only an MBA. Moreover, the fluidity of the private higher education environment makes it likely that a snapshot of any point in time will likely be quickly out of date. Unless indicated otherwise, the numbers included here are from Dubai's Knowledge and Human Development Authority (KHDA) as of May 2010.

The rapid buildup of private higher education in Dubai reflects a broader recognition by Gulf leaders that education, which had been severely underdeveloped for decades, is critical for the future development of the region. In 1985 access to postsecondary education in Dubai was nonexistent. Twenty-five years later, Dubai's KHDA reported that fifty postsecondary institutions were licensed to provide an associate's degree or higher in Dubai. Of those fifty institutions, three are campuses of the federal public institutions (Zayed University, Dubai Men's College, and Dubai's Women's College). Thus, forty-seven private (nonfederal) institutions operate in Dubai.

Of the institutions the KHDA currently recognizes, the Islamic and Arabic Studies College (IASC) is the oldest, first operating in the late 1980s and now providing bachelor's, master's, and doctoral programs in Islamic-based studies. It was established as a private philanthropic institution funded as a religious endowment. The IASC was soon joined by the two federally supported HCT campuses and the Dubai Pharmacy School. The first outpost of a foreign education provider, the University of Wollongong in Dubai (UOWD) from Australia, opened its doors in 1993, providing English language instruction. The UOWD has since grown into one of the largest private higher education universities in Dubai with a comprehensive academic offering, announcing the intent to add doctoral programs in business in 2010. The model of postsecondary education being provided by foreign institutions would expand as the leaders of Dubai began looking to emulate the developmental strategies of the west (Davidson and Smith, 2008) and would become the dominant form of private higher education expansion in Dubai.

Dubai's leader, Sheik Mohamed bin Rashid Al Maktoum, has been noted to have borrowed Tony Blair's famous slogan, "education, education, education," to express his awareness of the importance of education to the growth of his emirate (Gill, 2008). This emphasis by Sheik Mohamed, coupled with innovative public policies and the increase in the population during the last decade, has brought a massive expansion of the private higher education sector, with well over half of all private higher education institutions having opened in the last ten years. Most striking of the private higher education sector is that approximately half (twenty-five) of the campuses (as of January 2010) are physical outposts of a foreign-based institution (for example, Michigan State University–Dubai, Murdoch University–Dubai), part of a global multicampus structure (Hult University and INSEAD), or a portal to another country's higher education system (for example, the Canadian University of Dubai and the British University of Dubai).

From a programmatic perspective, two core developments in the private higher education sector should be noted. First, the expansion of the postsecondary educational pipeline has primarily occurred in the baccalaureate and master's levels, leaving limited opportunities at the associate and doctoral levels. The limited basic vocational training appears to be provided mostly by local providers. Indeed, only seven private institutions have been authorized to provide associate-level credentials, and with the exception of the Canadian University of Dubai, none of these institutions are foreign providers. A majority of all private institutions (thirty), however, provide graduate-level education in the form of master's degrees (twenty-two of which are offered by a foreign education provider), and four institutions are licensed by the KHDA to offer doctoral degrees (the British University in Dubai, Exeter University in Dubai, Islamic and Arabic Studies College, Murdoch University). Twenty-eight private institutions provide baccalaureate-level programs.

Second, demonstrating the market-based orientation of most private higher education institutions, academic program development largely reflects the fact that job growth has primarily been in business and real estate (Dubai Statistics Center, 2008). Almost all graduate and undergraduate programs are focused on the professions (for example, business, engineering, education). An analysis of the program titles reveals that many of them also serve as descriptors of the areas that were driving the Dubai economy at the beginning of the twenty-first century: construction management, property development and management, media and mass communications, entrepreneurship, and so forth. In fact, more than three-fifths of all institutions (twenty-one) offer at least one business-related master's degree program, and five of those institutions offer an executive MBA program. Comparatively, programs in the arts, humanities, and social sciences are almost nonexistent in both the public and private sectors. Exceptions are largely in the area of local cultural studies such as those at the America University of Dubai and the Islamic and Arabic Studies College–Dubai. Middlesex University–Dubai offers degrees in global social science and psychology, and the SAE University–Dubai has several arts-oriented programs. These programs all have a professional orientation, however, with the programs at the SAE focusing on careers in the film, audio, and multimedia industries.

Economic Development, Regulation, and Dubai's Private Higher Education Sector

Private higher education in Dubai, which has been one of the Middle East's fastest-growing financial capitals, is closely tied to the emirate's economy and economic policies. Indeed, the patchwork that is the private higher education sector in Dubai is primarily the result of developments in the emirate's economic development policy in the 1980s and 1990s (Lane, forthcoming). Like many developing nations, the UAE has a set of federal protectionist laws that require corporations and educational institutions operating in the UAE to be primarily locally owned and governed (Davidson, 2008). To attract more foreign business to their land, Dubai established free zones, which are governed by special authorities (Davidson, 2008; Excelencia Free Zone, 2008). These free zones exempt corporations that operate within their borders from federal regulations, including the Commercial Companies Law and federal quality assurance requirements (Wilkins, 2001). They can also retain 100 percent ownership of the business, repatriate all capital and profits, and are exempt from all commercial, including export and import, levies. More than half (thirty) of the private higher education institutions operate in one of Dubai's free zones.

The most widely known free zones dealing with private higher education are the Dubai Knowledge Village (DKV) and the Dubai International

Academic City (DIAC), likely because their names imply a focus on higher education and their mission has been to attract foreign education providers to Dubai. They are not the only free zones with campuses operating within their borders, however. Other free zones (for example, the Dubai International Financial City, the Dubai Health Care City, and the Silicone Oasis) have attracted higher education institutions as part of their research and development strategy. For example, Boston University's Institute for Dental Research and Education is located in Dubai Health Care City, and the Dubai International Financial City hosts the London Business School and other leading business programs.

Importantly, the free zones are tools for economic and property development, not government entities designed to coordinate the growth of private higher education. For example, the DKV and the DIAC are property developments owned by TECOM, a subsidiary of Dubai Holding. It does not mean that the institutions operating in the free zones do not help fulfill public policies or that the leaders of these entities do not coordinate with government officials. It does mean, however, that government coordination and regulation of the private higher education sector's development has been limited, particularly from the federal government. Use of the free zones to expand higher education has resulted in a dualistic regulatory environment. Although federal law requires all nonfederal public institutions to be licensed by the Commission on Academic Accreditation (CAA), the free zones exempt the universities operating in their borders from this requirement. Thus until recently, institutions in these free zones developed with very little local regulation. Coordinated regulation of the free zones, and all of Dubai for that matter, has begun under the auspices of the KHDA. Before establishment of the KHDA, the independent authorities that governed each free zone retained the power to determine the criteria under which a private higher education institution could be established in the free zone. Although authorities still have a great deal of autonomy to determine which institutions may open in the free zone, all private higher education institutions in Dubai must be licensed by the KHDA through the University Quality Assurance International Board. The UQAIB was designed to ensure that branch campuses are approved and accredited in the home country and that the branch and its programs are "equivalent" to the home campus and its programs. At the time of this writing, the UQAIB was undergoing its first full round of institutional evaluations.

Although the dual system was meant to encourage the development and growth of foreign private higher education providers, emerging tensions are beginning to affect the operations of foreign providers. Free zones allow home campuses to retain control over the campuses, including provision of academic programs and admission standards, as well as exempt them from having to abide by CAA requirements such as the governing board's including "representatives of the [local] community" and requiring all graduates to have completed a course in Islamic studies, history, or culture (Commission on Academic Accreditation, 2010, sections 2.5.1 and 3.5.2). Emirati students who attend non-CAA-licensed institutions, however, cannot use the very generous financial aid provided by the government through local foundations and are restricted from government employment, where many of the most coveted jobs exist. These later issues make it difficult for some institutions to recruit local students. Impediments to recruiting local students become more apparent with the current economic downturn, causing a shrinking pool of students from which these mostly enrollment-financed institutions draw.

The Role of Private Higher Education in Dubai

Lane (forthcoming) analyzed the development of IBCs in Dubai. His analysis is adapted and expanded here to include all private higher education institutions in Dubai.

The growth of private higher education in Dubai follows similar developmental patterns seen in other areas of the globe, although the use of free zones has fostered dimensions of growth not seen elsewhere. Levy's framework for studying the growth of private higher education (1986) suggests that private higher education institutions develop to provide something superior to what is already provided, something different from what is provided, or something more for students unable to study within the existing system. These divisions are helpful in understanding how private higher education has evolved in Dubai over the last twenty-five years.

Attracting institutions from nations with prestigious higher education systems has been a part of the emirate's desire to increase its global awareness of its educational offerings and become a regional educational hub. In Dubai, the pursuit of superiority comes not so much from institutions but from the system. As such, rather than investing only in local institutions, educational decision makers in Dubai have been working to tap into the prestige of existing institutions and systems with global recognition. Private higher education institutions in Dubai with the most global recognition are the outposts of highly ranked institutions such as Boston University, London Business School, and Michigan State University. Further, although most IBCs are not considered elite institutions, most do come from leading importers of foreign students (Australia, the United Kingdom, and the United States, for example) (Becker, 2009).

The provision of something different is the second significant motivator in the expansion of private higher education. Globally, the development of something different often translates into the expansion of religious-based institutions, which has also been the case in Dubai. Many locally supported institutions provide access to programs focused on Islamic-focused programs (such as Shariah finance or Islamic studies) or providing programs taught in an Islamic-grounded environment. The expansion of IBCs, however, has brought a variety of differences, most of which are based on the geographic location of the home campus. The existence of IBCs allows students to decide whether they want to engage in an American-, Australian-, or British-style educational experience, for example. Thus, these institutions provide students the opportunity to select among different types of academic programs, instructional provision, and student culture. Although much of private higher education globally has occurred to absorb demand, the private higher education system in Dubai seems to be shifting from demand absorption to demand creation, a trend just recently documented (Lane, 2010a). Because public education is limited to only national citizens, a number of domestic and foreign institutions have opened to serve the children of the growing expatriate population in Dubai. For example, American University in Dubai, one of the largest private higher education providers, exemplifies the large expatriate enrollments that exist even in domestically rooted institutions. Founded in 1995, the school enrolled almost 3,000 students in fall 2008 (American University in Dubai, 2009). Of those students enrolled, fewer than 20 percent were reported to be UAE nationals; the other students are expatriates representing 85 different nationalities from around the world. Similarly, institutions such as the Birla Institute of Technology and Science–Pilani and Manipal University are branches of Indian-based institutions that serve, although not exclusively, the local Indian expatriate community in the UAE.

In addition to serving the local populations, Dubai has indicated that it wants to become a regional hub for higher education (Verbik and Lasanowski, 2007). Because public education is restricted to emirati students, private higher education is crucial for the realization of this goal. In fact, a recent statement by the executive director of the DIAC, Dr. Ayoub Kazim, makes clear his vision for using IBCs to attract students from around the region: "DIAC is committed to developing the education sector and offering the region innovative academic choices. By offering leading education infrastructure to our academic partners, we aim to contribute to the advancement of the human capital of the UAE and the region through the development of quality graduates" (Dubai International Academic City, 2010). Thus, the private higher education sector is meant to serve local students as well as to help expand local educational capacity so that Dubai can attract more students from throughout the region. The strategy being pursued is to provide an array of options, not only different academic programs but also institutions with varying levels of prestige from a range of different countries.

Opportunities and Challenges for the Future

Dubai has emerged as a leader by using foreign institutions to grow its higher education sector. Whether or not this development strategy will pay off as hoped is yet to be seen. Current and historical data about student enrollment patterns are very limited and idiosyncratic. Dubai docs, however, represent a group of states whose policies are challenging the traditional models of the growth of private higher education. The system is growing not through the evolution of local institutions but by the importation of mostly name-brand institutions from other countries to serve the large local expatriate population and in the hope of actualizing a supply-driven development strategy—if you build it, they will come. The question now is whether these IBCs can survive the global economic recession, which has had significant effects on Dubai and its population.

Because of its tight alignment with the local economy, the health of the private higher education sector is closely tied to the health of the local economy. The public sector receives almost all of its funding from the government, and students are almost all from UAE nations. Although Dubai is trying to attract more students from other countries, however, the enrollments of most private higher education institutions, domestic and foreign, largely comprise students who have economic rather than cultural or historical ties to the area. Thus, if the economy shrinks, the pool of students is likely to shrink as expatriate families relocate out of Dubai and prospective employment opportunities decrease. Alternatively, Dubai's relatively liberal policies for foreign institutions to establish a local presence and proximity to countries such as India (with its excess demand for higher education) could provide Dubai with the opportunity to develop into a more regional educational hub, although it does face competition from other nations seeking to become regional hubs such as Qatar, Malaysia, and Singapore (Kinser and Lane, 2010) as well as grow private higher education in neighboring emirates.

Even though 2009 ended with Dubai unable to pay off all of its debt as a result of the significant decline in property prices and foreign investment, great optimism remains in the emirate for the future. The beginning of 2010 saw Dubai rush to open the Burj Khalifa, the world's tallest building—in part to change the story being told. A briefing in the *Economist,* however, noted that the opening of significant skyscrapers has historically marked the end of a financial boom, not the beginning. This unscientific diagnosis of bursting bubbles raises comparisons of a similar phenomenon in the 1980s, when Japan's higher education system expanded significantly through the creation of IBCs in the midst of its economic bubble (see Croom, forthcoming). All but one of those institutions are now closed.

Given the current economic downturn in Dubai, one can only wait to see whether its branch campuses will suffer a similar fate. Many of the current private higher education institutions decided to invest in a Dubai campus in the midst of Dubai's massive economic expansion, when the number of expatriates, employment opportunities, and salaries were growing. The unanticipated collapse of the student market could affect the success of these efforts.

Dubai saw a handful of branch campuses close their doors in 2009 (information about closures of domestic institutions is not available). Weak enrollments caused in part by the global recession may cause more to close or restructure their offerings. This situation could have the unfortunate result of losing high-quality programs that were not able to build a solid foundation and so weather such a significant economic storm. Well-established schools such as the University of Wollongong and the American University in Dubai will likely survive relatively unscathed, as they have a proven history and institutionalized brand recognition. Many of the IBCs, though, have not existed long enough to graduate any students. Though they may have an internationally recognized brand, they are not yet part of the local culture. Many of these institutions are still operating as start-ups, trying to figure out how best to recruit, retain, and graduate students. Moreover, many students are still waiting to see whether these institutions will be around long enough for them to earn a degree.

Public Policy and the Growth of Private Higher Education in Thailand

THE THAI HIGHER EDUCATION SYSTEM is dominated by the public sector, whereas the private sector has existed for centuries in elementary-secondary education, vocational education, and social welfare. Historically, both sectors are sharply different in their geneses and roles, leading to the sectoral dynamics of the system's development.

During the first half of the twentieth century, only public universities were permitted. The state's Commission on Higher Education (CHE) solely controlled the system's governance, finance, and function. Especially before 1973, Thailand's military-bureaucratic force was prominent, leading the country into political modernization with major support from the United States to strengthen market economy and technocratic training (Chaloemtiarana, 1979; Darling, 1962; Fineman, 1997; Hussey, 1993). Such state-led power became one of associated factors for public universities to mushroom.

Unlike its public predecessor, the private sector became formalized because of exceeding demand for higher education that public universities could not accommodate. The 1969 Private College Act was promulgated, bestowing "college" status to the first six private institutions (Bangkok College, Pattana College, DhurakijPundit College, Kirk College, Sripatum College, and Thai Chamber of Commerce College). Originally restricted to only associate's degrees, later permission was extended—with rigid controls—for them to offer bachelor's degrees (Boonprasert, 2002; Bureau of Policy and Planning, 2003; Kulachol, 1995; Watson, 1991). Such rigid control for private higher

The primary responsibility for developing this chapter was taken by Prachayani Praphamontripong.

education institutions demonstrates typical Asian patterns. In Thailand, the Private Higher Education Act and ministerial regulations have been reauthorized gradually through the legislative process; private higher education institutions have been slowly given a certain degree of institutional autonomy.

Through the perspective of institutional diversity, this chapter discusses the growth of Thai higher education with a particular focus on the private side and highlights two crucial government policies—the Private Higher Education Act and student loans—that have facilitated private growth.

The Growth of Private Higher Education and Institutional Diversity

When compared with the traditional public higher education sector created in 1917, the private sector has grown since 1969, though Table 3 shows its percentage of enrollments held stagnant in the early decades of its genesis. During those first two decades, government regulations for private higher education were rigid, thereby allowing less room for the private sector to penetrate the sector (Kulachol, 1995). The rationale for passing private higher education laws was therefore not the growing significance of private higher education institutions but the *rapid* proliferation of private higher education in Thailand in the 1990s.

The growth of Thai private higher education during the 1990s to early 2000s may be explained in part by the political economic events during that period. The 1992 coup d'état almost dissolved the ruling military's power; consequently, the 1995 election decreased the number of military senators and replaced them with businessmen. The 1997 Asian economic crisis forced Thailand to open itself to trade under the conditions of the International Monetary Fund (Friedman, 2000; Phongpaichit and Baker, 2002). Also during 1997 to 2000, the democratic government promulgated many laws concerning economic liberalization; among such laws was the 1998 Student Loan Funds Act. Accordingly, a window of opportunity was opened to private providers, especially for "proprietary" institutions (which in Thailand are legally not for profit, even when licensed by a proprietor). Furthermore, during 2001 to 2006, the Thai-rak-Thai government, with strong political and economic networks, had

TABLE 3
Comparison of Private and Public Growth in Thai Higher Education

Year	Total Number of Higher Education Institutions	Total Number of Public Higher Education Institutions	Total Number of Private Higher Education Institutions	Total Private Higher Education Institutions (Percent)	Total Number of Higher Education Enrollment	Total Enrollment Number in Public Higher Education Institutions	Total Enrollment Number in Private Higher Education Institutions	Total Private Higher Education Enrollment (Percent)
1972	17	11	6	35.3	67,848	63,823	4,025	5.9
1976	23	13	10	43.5	175,418	161,363	14,055	8.0
1981	25	14	11	44.0	670,829	639,798	31,031	4.6
1986	35	16	19	54.3	728,615	675,480	53,135	7.3
1991	46	21	25	54.3	629,498	518,956	110,542	17.6
1996	57	22	35	61.4	904,636	730,876	173,760	19.2
2001	75	24	51	68.0	1,179,569	955,759	223,810	19.0
2006	143	78	65	45.5	2,106,869	1,830,146	276,723	13.1

Note: Intervals of years are organized using the Thai B.E. year (starting from B.E. 2515). Data of public community colleges have been excluded, given that the community college sector is relatively new to Thailand.

Source: Praphamontripong, 2010.

overwhelmingly promoted various national policies supporting the private sector, not just in education but in other areas as well (McCargo and Pathmanand, 2005; Phongpaichit and Baker, 2004). Under this government, the 2003 Private Higher Education Act was reauthorized with much more flexible regulations than the previous laws (although, as indicated later, still plenty of regulations to follow).

A drastic diversification in the public sector during 2001 to 2006 appeared as well. All Rajabhat public institutes (founded as teachers colleges) and Rajamangla public institutes of technology were upgraded to universities and transferred to the CHE, resulting in an enormous expansion in the public sector. Such political upgrades may in part explain the renewed stagnancy in the percentage of private enrollments since 2003. Indeed, the public sector has consistently shared roughly 80 percent of the total higher education enrollments. Table 3 reflects a multidimensional growth pattern, with a few new private higher education institutions founded where there once had been public dominance. Growth in private higher education mushroomed after facilitating legislative during the late 1990s, followed in the public sector in the early 2000s through an extreme expansion of the Rajabhat University system, the Rajamangla University system, traditional limited admission (competitive) universities, and autonomous universities.

Intrasector Growth: Types of Private Higher Education

The Thai private sector comprises three institutional types—university, college, and institute—designated in the Private Higher Education Act. Even so, such a categorization represents a superficial portrayal of the reality of Thai private higher education institutions because mobility in institutional status (for example, from college to university) often occurs (Praphamontripong, 2008a).

Levy's private higher education typology (religious oriented, elite, demand absorbing) (1986) is appropriate, as Thai private higher education is entrenched in both religious and business organizations. Since 1567 Christianity has engaged in private elementary and secondary education and western-style medical education (Matawatsarapak, 2001), whereas business associations have played a significant role in public policy since the early 1980s

(Laothamatas, 1992). Although this typology mostly holds valid in the case of Thailand, it requires multiple adaptations. "Religious oriented" is extended to religious and cultural oriented, for Thailand has many higher education institutions founded by religious sects—Catholic, Christian, Islamic, Buddhist—as well as culturally based ones. "Elite" is reinterpreted as "semielite," as none of the prestigious private universities qualify for the traditional elite definitions. "Demand absorbing" also involves an exception: whereas previous studies confirm that this type normally emerges later than others (Levy, 1986; Silas Casillas, 2005), the Thai illustration shows an overlapping emergence with a large proportion of demand-absorbing private higher education institutions of recent vintage, while a few emerged long before.

Religious and cultural orientation. In Thailand, diversity in the religious, culturally oriented subsector reflects the interests of various religious orientations and cultural groups in supporting higher education. Christian and Catholic universities emerged first, Islamic and Buddhist ones much later. Except for Payap University, which offers a comprehensive curriculum, other small Christian-oriented institutions often aim at religious fields alongside nursing and the health sciences. In particular, Saengtham College, founded in 1975, exclusively focuses on training prospective priests. Islamic and Buddhist colleges are recent, small, and narrow in their orientations. Regardless of denomination, most religion-oriented private higher education institutions are governed by priests or religious members sent by the founders; many university presidents are indeed priests or nuns. Some institutions are also attached to their religious founders through a financial system. As to cultural institutions, they have been founded recently and are very specialized. Examples include Arsomsilp Institute of the Arts and Development and Thai-Nichi Institute of Technology. These institutions are not religious but are cultural in their thrust, similar to institutions in central Europe. Such growing religious and cultural orientation in private higher education signifies great intrasectoral diversity, with differences stemming from different types of religious orders and founders, various missions and emphases, and institutional size.

The idea of a religious subsector comprising more than one religion alongside a few exceptional cases is embryonic in the private higher education literature. The Thai case should not therefore be considered typical. Whether these various religiously oriented institutions are more likely to harmonize, ignore, or compete with one another needs further investigation (Otieno and Levy, 2007).

Semielite. Illustrations of academic elite private institutions outside the United States are unusual. Consequently, the word "semielite" refers to private higher education institutions "between elite and non-elite" (Demurat, 2008; Levy, 2008a; Praphamontripong, 2008b; Silas Casillas, 2008). They are leading institutions in their own countries with several indicators of prestige, including high-profile students, a reputation comparable with most good public universities, niche and business orientations, trendiness in internationalism, and entrepreneur and well-tuned employment networks.

Still, applying the global concept one can hardly find semielite private higher education institutions in Thailand. Out of almost seventy private higher education institutions, very few are considered semielite. They are top private universities holding the highest national reputation among private higher education institutions. Their founding licensees are mostly affluent families or private companies, partly echoing Levy's determination that semielite private higher education institutions are often founded by wealthy philanthropists or elitists. Indeed, in Thailand their founders are among private higher education leaders who influenced the government on the promulgation of the first private higher education law.

The literature suggests that semielite institutions tend to be recently founded and small (Levy, 2007a). Nevertheless, Thai semielite private higher education institutions are among the oldest and largest in the sector (also see the chapter on Bulgaria in this volume), comprising five institutions: Assumption University, Bangkok University, University of the Thai Chamber of Commerce, Dhurakij Pundit University, and Rangsit University (Praphamontripong, 2010). Rangsit is an exception, as its emergence was a few decades later. The five prototypes have held approximately 40 percent of the total private enrollment for decades. Furthermore, in Chongwibul's study (2001), these institutions especially aim to produce graduates for the business- and technologically-related industries networking with them. Their leaders and key professors are involved in the national policymaking process and in many international associations.

Demand absorbing. Like elsewhere, roughly 80 percent of Thai private higher education institutions are demand absorbing, sharing more than 50 percent of the total private enrollment. Echoing the private higher education literature (Altbach, 2005; Kinser, 2006), Thai demand-absorbing private higher education institutions are primarily family owned. A majority of them are relatively new and small, established after 1991. Indeed, small demand-absorbing colleges mushroomed after enactment of the 1998 Student Loans Fund Act. Exceptions are apparent, however; a few are almost as old and comprehensive as their semielite counterparts.

Given their focus on low-cost programs such as accounting, business administration, law, and professional training, demand-absorbing institutions are often viewed suspiciously for their academic quality and financial management (Geiger, 1991; Gellert and Rau, 1992; Levy, 2006). Because they are family oriented, their institutional administration tends to be centralized, with minimum transparency along the financial continuum. Thai demand-absorbing private higher education institutions claim to provide academic training in the high-demand fields that respond to society's needs. Such a claimed mission is not so different from that of the semielites, except that semielites also claim national research and academic distinction. Although demand-absorbing institutions *actually* function according to their name, "demand absorbers," particularly small colleges, report that they do not see or call themselves demand absorbing. Instead, they positively claim their devotion for second-class or needy students who cannot otherwise get into well-established private or public universities. Their strengths thus lie on good caring and close relationships between faculty and students. In the demand-absorbing subsector, however, Thai findings show a glimpse of a separate pattern, explored in recent private higher education literature as "serious demand absorbing" (Levy, 2007b). Several demand-absorbing private higher education institutions appear to be gaining some degree of national reputation—but not so high as the semielites—focused as they are on a particular niche and well connected to a particular marketplace (Praphamontripong, 2010). In this sense, they may fit the profile of serious demand absorbing, thereby making the subsector even more diversified.

Public Policy Facilitating Private Growth

Public policy has become a crucial agenda in many countries where the focus is on private sector regulation (Neave and van Vught, 1994). Although Thai private higher education institutions have received none of the government's funding for their annual operations, they are strictly subject to the Private Higher Education Act and abundant ministerial regulations under the CHE's supervision (Kulachol, 1995). Among such policies, the two major ones influencing the growth of Thai private higher education are the Private Higher Education Act and income-contingent student loans.

Private Higher Education Act and Ministerial Regulations

The Private Higher Education Act is the most fundamental law applying directly to all Thai private higher education institutions since 1969. Public universities, in contrast, have their individual statutes, which tends to allow them to enjoy their autonomy from the government much more than do private higher education institutions (see the chapter on Kenya for a similar feature). Accordingly, conflicts on favoritism and dissimilar treatment of the government toward the private and public institutions are often discoursed, leading to reauthorization of the Private Higher Education Act several times.

The latest law is the Private Higher Education Act B.E. 2546, enacted in 2003, supplemented by the Second Private Higher Education Act B.E. 2550, released in 2007. Act 2550 is considered the less rigid one with regard to private higher education institutions, which are supposed to enjoy equal status similar to that of the public universities and to exercise abundant autonomy under their own university councils' authority, with the CHE being only a postauditor.

The most significant change enforced by Act 2550 is that private and public higher education institutions are now subject to similar educational standards assessed by the CHE and the Office for National Education Standards and Quality Assessment. The university council of private and public higher education institutions, under the CHE's acknowledgment, has power to approve curricula and confer degrees and to act as administrator in various university affairs. Before Act 2550, most academic affairs for private higher education institutions—such as launching a new curriculum, changing course numbers and contents of examinations, and approving degrees—had to be approved by the CHE. Even semielite institutions found difficulty in keeping up with such rigidity. Furthermore, although the law governs all private higher education institutions similarly regardless of their types, different private higher education institutions tend to receive different impacts from the law. Because the law contains high standards, large and long-standing private universities with high capacity (that is, the semielites and serious demand absorbers) may fulfill such requirements much easier than small family-owned demand-absorbing colleges with limited resources. Nevertheless, by bestowing the power to the university council, Act 2550 seems to officially loosen up the government's rigid control over private higher education institutions. With this act, the Thai government proclaims its justice in giving private higher education institutions sufficient institutional autonomy, similar to the treatment of public universities.

Alongside the Private Higher Education Act are more than twenty ministerial regulations governing private higher education institutions. Such regulations cover various procedural issues such as specification of lands; conditions for institutional establishment; institutional accreditation; procedures on declaring institutional property and donations; curricula and programs; degree conferral; faculty appointment; faculty standards; employee benefits and fringes; design of identification cards for employees; faculty, employee, and student databases; changes of institutional status or name; branch campuses; accounting and annual financial report, advertising procedures; and the annual report (Bureau of Legal Affairs, 2007). Even with Act 2550 and its subsequent freedoms, private higher education institutions still fight the overwhelming regulations. Small private colleges, particularly demand-absorbing and religious-oriented ones, tend to suffer more than semielite universities. Semielites, with their certain reputations, have some informal discretion explicitly acknowledged, as their leaders and eminent professors serve on various national committees. They are wealthier, thereby having abundant resources to fulfill the regulations more easily. As Trow (1987) stressed, leading universities such as elite private institutions tend to have the best of everything—students, faculty members, resources, alumni, and reputations. Their voices are normally heard in public policy discourses, leaving behind other less-developed institutions. Such is the case in Thailand.

Government Student Loan Programs

Thailand is no exception to the globally popular higher education loan schemes. Since the 1997 economic crisis and as part of its economic liberalization commitment to the International Monetary Fund, Thailand revised its student loan fund policy in 1998 to ensure access for needy students through student loans under excessively favorable repayment conditions (Ziderman, 2003). Another type of student loan—income-contingent loans—were introduced in 2006 and are modeled after the successful Australian program (Chapman, 2005; Ziderman, 2006). The loans are given to students in both private and public higher education institutions who meet specified requirements. Both the student loan fund and income-contingent loans have become a prime income source for private higher education institutions in the form of tuition and fees. The degree of private higher education institutions' financial dependency on the government through student loans, however, varies among private higher education types, and the student loan programs facilitate different kinds of private higher education expansion.

With the policy on student loans, students from any higher education institution can apply for government loans. Certain restrictions apply, however, as the government's budget is limited. Loans are need based, limited to high school students applying to a higher education institution, vocational education students, and baccalaureate and undergraduate students whose family's annual income does not exceed $5,714. The amount given to each student varies by the student's field of study, ranging from $2,400 for social science and architecture to $4,971 for medicine, veterinary medicine, and dentistry.[1] Two years after graduating, students must start paying back the loan at 1 percent interest for a maximum of fifteen years.

This loan, while helpful to most, limits its pool of applicants and may be unfair in its dispersal of funds. The loan allocation to higher education institutions is based on number of students. More importantly, this loan scheme has expanded very quickly, resulting in budgetary cutbacks. Eventually, each individual institution will receive minimum loan amounts below recommended levels.

Income-contingent loans, in contrast, are based on a cost-sharing platform, moving beyond the previous state-subsidized social platform. This loan scheme is restricted to only baccalaureate and undergraduate students of certain majors that support the government's needs. The amount of loans awarded per year varies with the field of study, from social science and architecture ($1,714) to medicine, veterinary medicine, and dentistry ($4,285). Although the procedure for paying back a loan is relatively similar to that for the student loan fund, tax authorities are responsible for collecting payments (Ziderman, 2006). This loan is even more selective, as it can fluctuate depending on the government's needs, and the coverage specified at the moment may change based on market demand. Although student loans and income-contingent loans are available for both private and public higher education institutions, the loans help lessen the financial burden of private higher education institutions more than they help the public universities because public universities already charge tuition and fees at a subsidized rate. Apparently, government student loans help a great deal in facilitating the expansion of private higher education institutions. Private higher education institutions typically receive government subsidies by enrolling students whose tuition is paid by the government (World Bank, 2000). Students who cannot afford higher education on their own can have money through the loans to pay tuition and fees at a private higher education institution.

Echoing global reality, Table 4 shows that Thai demand absorbers tend to bank on such student loans the most, whereas a majority of semielites rely on student loans the least. Some serious-demand-absorbing institutions rely substantially on income-contingent loans, as most of their students are qualified for the fields particularly promoted. Other serious-demand-absorbing ones intentionally receive fewer loans as they already provide their own institutional scholarships. Semielite institutions also have other sources of income aside from student loans, thereby accepting fewer loans.

Some institutional discrepancies are revealed as a result of the loans. It is believed that in being considered for the loans, small demand-absorbing

TABLE 4
Different Types of Thai Private Higher Education Institutions (PHEIs) Receiving Student Loans

PHEIs	Students Receiving Student Loans	Percent of Total Income from Tuition and Fees
Semielite		
Institution A	Less than 10%	About 80%
Institution B	Less than 15%	About 90%
Institution L	About 30%	About 90%
Institution Q	About 30%	N/A
Institution D	About 60%	About 90%
Serious Demand Absorbing		
Institution M	Less than 10%	About 50%
Institution J	About 30%	About 80%
Institution E	About 60%	About 80%
Institution F	About 80%	About 90%
Religious Oriented		
Institution N	About 60%	About 70%
Demand Absorbing		
Institution R	About 60%	About 95%
Institution P	About 70%	About 98%
Institution K	More than 80%	About 90%

Note: This table illustrates thirteen different private higher education institutions in four categories that receive student loan funds or ICL (Income Contingent Loan) or both. The percentages are estimates given by interviewees of each institution.

Source: Praphamontripong, 2010.

private colleges are treated less favorably than public universities and large private universities, even if the latter ones do not necessarily need the loans so much as the former. This situation has become problematic for the higher education system as a whole. Some institutions vigorously recruit students eligible for the loans through aggressive advertising, sometimes resulting in scandals, thus creating misunderstandings and conflicts among different sectors of higher education. Therefore, to ameliorate a rivalry, Ziderman (2003) suggested that any loan scheme needs simultaneous consideration on the issues of planning, monitoring, execution, evaluation, and organizational structure at both the macro and institutional system levels.

Conclusion and Trends

The Thai case typifies a global tendency in developing countries in which higher education overall expands, especially in private higher education. The surge in the private higher education share is pronounced in the institutional counts, as public institution numbers either stagnate or rise more modestly than private institution numbers. Aside from rising demand for higher education, dissatisfaction with public universities as a result of political agitation and mediocre academic quality may boost the growth of institutional counts in the private sector (World Bank, 2002). Other Asian examples of the institutional surge in private higher education include Bangladesh, China, Indonesia, Malaysia, and Mongolia. In the private sector, different types of Thai private higher education institutions continue to expand, mostly in absolute numbers rather than in enrollment share. The demand-absorbing subsector is burgeoning as a majority in institutional numbers, while the semielite subsector is dominant in enrollment share. Culturally oriented private higher education institutions are growing in numbers as well. Apparently Levy's typology, with necessary adaptations, accurately depicts a picture of growth and diversity in Thai private higher education, with some private higher education institutions showing characteristic mixtures among the three types. For example, Assumption University is fundamentally oriented toward religion but it portrays semielite characteristics much stronger than its religious characteristics. Assumption University is thus exceptional, illustrating a hybrid of religious and semielite orientations. Likewise, Payap University is also fundamentally religion oriented while simultaneously demonstrating several characteristics of serious-demand-absorbing private higher education institutions. It has a certain national reputation and niches in humanities and social sciences. Payap University, hence, shows a mix between religious and serious-demand-absorbing orientation.

Last, external factors facilitating the growth in Thai private higher education also play a part. Along with the market economy, policy initiatives responding to privatization and diversification work to shape the transformation of private higher education (Fisher and others, 2004; Mei, 2002; Ntshoe, 2004). In Thailand, the Private Higher Education Act and government student loan programs are among the most important factors affecting the expansion of private higher education. Although competition for legitimacy and funding is increasingly aggressive, small demand-absorbing colleges are merging and closing. Another sign is that private higher education institutions are trying to differentiate themselves from others, as often seen in the serious-demand-absorbing subsector. Thai private higher education has illustrated various and globally relevant mixes of conflict, competition, and cooperation in both inter- and intrasector higher education.

Recent Patterns in the Growth of Private Higher Education in the United States

THIS CHAPTER REPORTS ON RECENT DEVELOPMENTS in private higher education enrollments, market share, and numbers of institutions in the United States. They are basic indicators of the current health and service level of this sector, which has a venerable history in the United States. The main focus is a national overview with attention to the recently robust private for-profit sector as well as the much better known private non-profit institutional sector. The analysis examines enrollment growth patterns by such variables as full-time versus part-time students, graduate (including first-professional) enrollments compared with undergraduates, institutional size (at the outset of the period under study), and type of institution. Data are also presented on regional patterns of enrollment growth in the private sector. The aim is to provide a broad account of the relative successes and problems of different types of private institutions in the most recent decade and to offer at least preliminary ideas about factors that may have been important in determining these outcomes. Some speculative discussion is offered about what may be in store for American private higher education in the future.

Unlike most other countries, higher education in the United States is primarily a state policy function, not a national one. The national government has some important functions in higher education, namely being the largest provider of financial aid to students for college expenses—aid that is tenable at accredited private colleges—and being the major supporter of academic

The primary responsibility for developing this chapter was taken by William Zumeta and Robin Lasota.

research. Of the nation's nearly 4,350 accredited degree-granting colleges and universities, more than 1,600 are private nonprofit institutions and more than 1,000 are operated for profit. States are responsible for seeing to the education of their population, whether through public colleges and universities or, to a greater or lesser extent, the encouragement and oversight of private institutions (Zumeta, 2005). Thus, variation in policies across the fifty states is likely to account for some part of regional and state differences in the fortunes of private higher education (Zumeta, 1992, 1996).

Data and Definitions

All the data reported herein come from analyses by coauthors Zumeta and LaSota of data from the U.S. Department of Education's Integrated Postsecondary Education Data System (IPEDS), which is based on annual reports by higher educational institutions that are mandated under the Higher Education Act for institutions participating in the federal student aid programs under the act. The designations in the IPEDS determine which institutions are public, private nonprofit, or private for-profit and classify them as to highest degree offered. To get a sense of recent developments, changes in enrollments and numbers of reporting institutions were examined over a period of 11 years, ending with the most recent year for which data were available (fall 2007). The initial year, 1996, was selected because of accessibility of the data files for that year and because an earlier study (Zumeta, 1999) spanned an adjacent period, 1980 to 1995, to which comparisons were drawn.

Factors at Work Since 1996

Several factors have changed that may alter the enrollment success and rates of attrition for institutions in the U.S. private higher education sector in the more recent period (1996–2007) compared with the years from 1980 through 1995. First, the basic demographics affecting higher education changed, with growth in the number of high school graduates resuming and the numbers in the younger adult population over 25 leveling off. This situation might well have led to some return to much of the sector's traditional focus on young, full-time students and undergraduates. On the other hand, the return to college of those in the labor market has been greatest for those with graduate degrees (U.S. Bureau of the Census, 2007), suggesting that graduate programs would likely continue to grow. With the exception of the dot-com bust recessionary period of the early 2000s, most of the years from 1996 through 2007 were prosperous ones, with the U.S. stock market gaining dramatically overall, which should have helped many families pay for the high cost of private college tuition and aiding private sector enrollments. Moreover, public higher education tuition rates in the four-year subsector increased substantially faster than those in the private four-year subsector during much of this period (College Board, 2008a, p. 9), a distinct change from the earlier era, when charges at private institution grew faster.

With their relatively high tuition rates, U.S. private colleges and universities are thought to be quite dependent on government student aid programs (grants and loans to students). Student aid from federal and state sources grew by more than 80 percent in constant dollars over the ten years ending in 2007–08 (College Board, 2008b, p. 6), but it was still not enough to match private sector tuition increases, which averaged more than 6 percent annually over the same period. Thus, private colleges and universities provided more than $29 billion in institutionally funded aid to students in 2007–08—up 78 percent in constant dollars over the ten years—and student debt increased more in the private than the public sector (College Board, 2008b, p. 11), suggesting that affordability of these schools was a serious issue for students and families. This affordability problem would be expected to affect private sector competitiveness. Thus, the factors likely to affect private enrollments over the period from 1996 to 2007 were a mixed lot, even with demographic trends and the stock market's performance generally favorable. Continued growth in tuition charges at rates far above the growth in incomes, layered atop charges that were already much higher than those of public institutions, however, clearly strained families' ability to pay and likely exerted a dampening effect on growth of private sector enrollment.

Finally, although this discussion applies to the prospects of the private non-profit institutional sector, the demand for more educated labor throughout much of the economy and the loosening of public policy strictures on for-profit institutions, particularly their acceptance by most of the regional accrediting bodies and their accession into eligibility for many states' student aid programs (Kelly, 2001; Kinser, 2006), suggests that these schools may well have grown strongly during the more recent period under study. The for-profits had been growing in the prior period, but their share of all enrollments nationally was under 2 percent in 1995.

National Overview: 1996–2007

The changes in private higher education reflect growing numbers of students, as well as the absolute numbers of institutions. Student status has also changed, reflecting new patterns of enrollment at graduate and undergraduate levels and with full-time and part-time attendance. Finally, there are differences by region that demonstrate variations in the national pattern.

Enrollment Changes by Sector

Table 5 shows the national story of enrollment changes over this eleven-year period for the various private and public subsectors of American higher education. Overall, higher education enrollments grew by 27.3 percent over this period, from 14.3 million to 18.2 million. The largest and best-known private subsector, nonprofit baccalaureate and higher degree–granting (or four-year) institutions, grew by 23.4 percent, to more than 3.5 million students. The eleven-year growth rate of this subsector outstripped that of the 1980–1995 (fifteen-year) period by a substantial margin (+15 percent). This "flagship" private subsector held its own against both public four-year institutions (+23.6 percent) and public two-year colleges (+20.4 percent), a notable accomplishment in the face of the much lower prices of the public schools. The tiny private nonprofit two-year sector lost more than half its aggregate enrollments and had only about 33,500 students nationwide by 2007, as this subsector, largely comprising limited vocationally oriented and "finishing" schools for women, evidently lost its long running battle with much less expensive community colleges and with cultural obsolescence. As the sector is now so tiny, it is largely ignored in the remainder of this chapter.

TABLE 5

Percentage Change in Total Fall Enrollments from 1996–2007 by Postsecondary Institution Sector

	Sum of All Std	Sum of All UG Std	Sum of All GR+FP Std	Sum of All FT Std	Sum of All FT UG Std	Sum of All FT GR+FP Std	Sum of All PT Std	Sum of All PT UG Std	Sum of All PT GR+FP Std
4-Yr Pvt NP									
1996	2,867,181	2,037,065	830,116	2,021,570	1,589,948	431,622	845,611	447,117	398,494
2007	3,537,521	2,436,841	1,100,680	2,643,107	2,033,663	609,444	894,414	403,178	491,236
	23.4%	19.6%	32.6%	30.7%	27.9%	41.2%	5.8%	−9.8%	23.3%
2-Yr Pvt NP									
1996	75,375	75,253	122	56,434	56,344	90	18,941	18,909	32
2007	33,486	33,486	0	21,295	21,295	0	12,191	12,191	0
	−55.6%	−55.5%	−100.0%	−62.3%	−62.2%	−100.0%	−35.6%	−35.5%	−100.0%
4-Yr Pvt FP									
1996	130,976	105,858	25,118	102,625	84,192	18,433	28,351	21,666	6,685
2007	925,873	735,536	190,337	689,251	561,560	127,691	236,622	173,976	62,646
	606.9%	594.8%	657.8%	571.6%	567.0%	592.7%	734.6%	703.0%	837.1%

(*Continued*)

TABLE 5 (*Continued*)

	Sum of All Std	Sum of All UG Std	Sum of All GR+FP Std	Sum of All FT Std	Sum of All FT UG Std	Sum of All FT GR+FP Std	Sum of All PT Std	Sum of All PT UG Std	Sum of All PT GR+FP Std
2-Yr Pvt FP									
1996	173,489	173,489	0	143,857	143,857	0	29,632	29,632	0
2007	260,325	260,325	0	229,158	229,158	0	31,167	31,167	0
	50.1%	50.1%	0.0%	59.3%	59.3%	0.0%	5.2%	5.2%	0.0%
4-Yr Public									
1996	5,787,490	4,607,321	1,180,169	4,088,189	3,538,560	549,629	1,699,301	1,068,761	630,540
2007	7,151,376	5,798,499	1,352,877	5,229,567	4,537,990	691,577	1,921,809	1,260,509	661,300
	23.6%	25.9%	14.6%	27.9%	28.2%	25.8%	13.1%	17.9%	4.9%
2-Yr Public									
1996	5,251,340	5,250,915	425	1,870,747	1,870,747	0	3,380,593	3,380,168	425
2007	6,324,119	6,323,810	309	2,442,140	2,442,038	102	3,881,979	3,881,772	207
	20.4%	20.4%	-27.3%	30.5%	30.5%	0.0%	14.8%	14.8%	-51.3%
1996 Total 14,285,851									
2007 Total 18,232,700									

Note: UG, undergraduate; GR, graduate; FP, first professional; FT, full-time; PT, part-time.

Source: Integrated Postsecondary Education Data System (IPEDS): 1996–97; 2007–08.

A dramatic development compared with the previous period that is apparent in the table is the surge in enrollment in private for-profit institutions. For-profit schools offering a two-year degree (usually the associate's degree) as their highest degree grew by half (50.1 percent) in aggregate enrollments, while those granting the bachelor's or graduate degrees (private for-profit four-year schools) grew by more than 600 percent. This latter subsector added close to 800,000 students over the eleven years, considerably more than the approximately 670,000 added by the private nonprofit four-year schools. This development is quite remarkable in American higher education. It was fueled by the huge growth of the University of Phoenix and other for-profit chains with multiple campuses (Kinser, 2007).

The net effect of these different sector growth rates was that the for-profits' share (four-year plus two-year for-profit schools) jumped by more than 4 percentage points over the eleven-year period, roughly tripling from 2.1 percent in 1996 to 6.5 percent of all U.S. students in 2007. Interestingly, this increase was mostly at the expense of the public sector, which lost 3.4 points of market share (to 73.9 percent of all enrollments in 2007), while the private nonprofit sector lost 1 percentage point, falling from 20.6 percent of U.S. enrollment total in 1996 to 19.6 percent in 2007.

Changes in Number of Institutions by Sector
During the period from 1980 to 1995, about one hundred private nonprofit institutions ceased operations, while almost as many emerged, leaving the total number of such institutions almost unchanged. Table 6 shows the comparable figures for 1996 and 2007. In the four-year nonprofit sector, the rate of both births and deaths evidently accelerated, and, unlike in the previous period, deaths exceeded births by a significant margin (162 to 142). Thus, in 2007, 1,531 four-year private nonprofit colleges and universities were operating, compared with 1,551 in 1996.

The most dramatic changes depicted in these data are the big gains in for-profit institutions, which increased from 614 in 1996 to 1,043 in 2007 as a result of net gains of 281 two-year and 227 four-year for-profit institutions. Just five public institutions did not appear in the 2007 IPEDS reports that were included in 1996, while ninety-one public institutions appeared

TABLE 6
Institutional Births and Deaths and Net Change from
1996–2007

Institution Sector	Number of Institutional Births	Number of Institutional Deaths	Net Change (Births-Deaths)	2007 Total Number
4-Yr Pvt NP	142	162	−20	1531
2-Yr Pvt NP	32	89	−57	92
4-Yr Pvt FP	239	12	227	490
2-Yr Pvt FP	293	12	281	553
4-Yr Public	16	2	14	648
2-Yr Public	75	3	72	1032
Grand Total	**797**	**280**	**517**	**4346**

Note: Because IPEDS institutional self-reports can vary from year to year, these counts should be regarded as approximations.
Source: Integrated Postsecondary Educational Data System (IPEDS); 1996–97; 2007–08.

in 2007 but not in 1996. Most of this net gain was in the public two-year sector.

Enrollment Changes by Student Status

As shown in Table 5, each sector's aggregate enrollment changes over the study period are broken down into changes by student status, that is, full time versus part time and undergraduate or graduate (including first professional). The first professional category includes law, medicine, and a small number of other health professions that, in the U.S. system, are pursued at the postbaccalaureate level. As expected, the private nonprofit four-year sector's enrollment gains were stronger for full-time students (+30.7 percent) than for part time students(+5.8 percent)—a sharp reversal from the earlier period's pattern, when the institutions sought to tap new markets because numbers of traditional-age young people (who are more likely to enroll full time) were falling off. The demographic turnaround is also reflected in the stronger gains in undergraduate enrollments in the more recent period, +19.6 percent over the eleven years from 1996 to 2007, compared with just +8.7 percent over the fifteen years from 1980 to 1995.

Yet consistent with the incentives in the modern "human capital economy," graduate enrollments grew even faster than undergraduate enrollments from 1996 to 2007 (+32.6 percent). At the graduate level, full-time students in private nonprofit colleges and universities increased by a robust 41.2 percent, and part-time students also gained fairly strongly, 23.3 percent. But at the undergraduate level, the difference was more dramatic, with full-time undergraduate numbers growing by 27.9 percent, while part-time undergraduates actually *declined* by 9.8 percent. Private nonprofit institutions as a group thus seem to prefer full-time students when they can recruit them, especially undergraduates.

Despite the differential percentage growth rates, in absolute terms the private nonprofit four-year institutions as a group actually saw bigger gains in undergraduates than graduate students in the recent period, by some 400,000 to 270,000. Still, graduate students as a percentage of this subsector's total enrollment continued the previous era's pattern of increase, gaining from just under 29 percent in 1996 to 31.1 percent in 2007. The nonprofit four-year subsector's historic bread-and-butter student group, full-time undergraduates, continued to form a clear, if declining, majority of its students (57.5 percent) in 2007.

Turning to the for-profit subsectors, one sees huge percentage growth rates in all categories for the four-year for-profits. In absolute terms, the bulk of this sector's enrollment gains were at the undergraduate level (79 percent of the total gain in students), but graduate student numbers grew at a somewhat greater percentage rate. In addition, the bulk of this sector's enrollment gains were in full-time students, although part-time enrollments grew at a greater rate. The two-year for-profit sector by definition has no graduate students, so all of its 50 percent enrollment growth over the eleven-year period was in undergraduates. Almost all of this growth was in full-time students, as numbers for part-time grew by only 5.2 percent, or just 1,500 students. In short, U.S. for-profit institutions at both levels enroll mostly students they define as "full-time," which may surprise many who have not examined this sector closely.

Enrollment Patterns by Region

In the United States, the presence of the private sector varies substantially by region. For this analysis, we used the eight standard census regions used by the

U.S. Census Bureau.[2] Notably, in none of the regions were enrollments in the private nonprofit sector for 1996 to 2007 truly weak; they ranged from gains of 9.7 percent in the New England region and 10.7 percent in the Southwest, to 25 percent in the Great Lakes region and just over 30 percent in the Plains and Southeast regions to a high of almost 40 percent in the rapidly growing Rocky Mountain states. In New England, the private nonprofit sector includes many elite institutions with little interest in large-scale growth, and the region's population growth was small. In the Southwest, the nonprofits faced strong competition from for-profits, especially the University of Phoenix, based in Arizona. By and large, in the four regions where the private nonprofits grew most (the Rocky Mountain region excepted), the private sector has long had a significant, though not dominant, presence and has shown considerable capacity to influence state policies (Zumeta, 1992), which may have worked to its benefit during this period. Indeed, in all four regions the private nonprofit sector's enrollment growth rate exceeded that of the public sector. As for the for-profit sector, the most striking point is how much of its national enrollment gains were concentrated in the Southwest. More than a third (295,000) of the national for-profit enrollment increase of 882,000 students from 1996 to 2007 occurred in this four-state region. All the other regions except New England also saw substantial gains in for-profit enrollments, with the largest gains in the Southeast (161,000), Plains (120,000), and Far West (89,000) regions. Together, these four regions accounted for more than three-fourths of the for-profit sector's national enrollment gain. In many states in these regions, the private nonprofit sector is not large, so the for-profits may in some respects be responding to unfilled market niches. In New England, where the private nonprofit sector dominates even the public higher education sector, the tiny for-profit sector gained just 7,000 students over the period, no doubt hampered by the nonprofits' dominance in reputation and influence.

Relative Success of Private Institutions of Different Sizes

In general, private higher education institutions tend to be considerably smaller than their public counterparts; in many cases it is by design, as they seek to offer a distinctive and personalized educational experience to students. Small institutions, however, if they are not well endowed financially have little margin for error in projecting student enrollments and thus tend to be at more risk when enrollments fluctuate. Among the 118 four-year private non-profit institutional deaths between 1996 and 2007 that could be classified by 1996 enrollment size, ninety enrolled fewer than 1,000 students in 1996. This number represents a considerable (6.7 percent) death rate among four-year nonprofit schools in this size category. In the next smallest enrollment category (1,000 to 2,499 students in 1996), the death rate was 2.5 percent; in the 2,500 to 4,999 range, 1.2 percent; and with more than 10,000 students, 1.1 percent. So, the expected pattern of more precarious survival chances among smaller institutions appears to hold.

Unlike during 1980 to 1995 when smaller institutions as a group performed strongly in terms of enrollment gains and the larger categories did not, in the more recent period percentage enrollment gains by size category did not differ markedly. Institutional attrition in the smaller size categories notwithstanding, no size category fared poorly in overall enrollment gains. Private nonprofit schools in the two smallest categories (under 1,000 students in 1996 and 1,000 to 2,499 from 1996 to 2007) and those in the medium to large size (5,000 to 9,999) each gained a bit more than 20 percent over the eleven years. Those with 2,500 to 4,999 students gained a bit less, 15.2 percent, and the largest group (10,000 students and up in 1996) grew the least but still gained 13 percent overall. All the size categories, including the smallest schools, saw graduate student numbers grow at a greater rate than undergraduates. Moreover, all the size categories saw numbers of full-time students grow at a fairly healthy pace (the lowest growth rate was 19 percent at the smallest nonprofit colleges), but numbers of part-time students fell in the three largest categories. Part-time students increased strongly (+34.6 percent) only at the smallest schools, many of which thus seemed to be pursuing a different student recruiting strategy from their larger counterparts. Finally, nonprofit institutions that did not exist in 1996 (or at least could not be identified in the IPEDS data for that year) and thus did not belong in any of the 1996 enrollment size categories, accounted for about 87,600 students in 2007, or about 13 percent of the private nonprofit sector's total enrollment gains over the period.

The patterns of gains by size group in 1996 for private four-year, for-profit institutions indicates that the schools of 1,000 to 2,499 students at the outset fared best. But the dramatic overall gains in this sector over the period means that the original size classes tell relatively little about the current configuration of the for-profit sector. Many more schools would certainly be in the larger size classes now than was the case in 1996, and hundreds of new institutions have been established since then. In total, these newly appearing institutions accounted for almost 341,000, or about 39 percent, of the for-profit sector's total enrollment gain of 882,000 from 1996 to 2007.

Enrollment Changes by Type of Institution

This analysis is based on the latest (2005) Carnegie basic classification, the standard source for meaningfully classifying U.S. colleges and universities by institution.[3] Within the private nonprofit sector, no Carnegie class shows a decline in enrollments and only one category, baccalaureate colleges–arts and sciences, shows an increase below 10 percent (+9.6 percent). This category is an important one for private institutions, representing the traditional liberal arts schools that include the best-known, smaller, primarily undergraduate colleges and roughly 10 percent of private nonprofit enrollments in 2007. Many of the relatively wealthy elite colleges in this group may not have sought much growth, so the modest aggregate enrollment gain is not particularly surprising. Full-time undergraduates in this Carnegie category increased at a greater pace than total enrollments, +12.5 percent, while part-time undergraduates dropped quite substantially, −36.2 percent, suggesting that these colleges no longer felt much need to enroll part-time students. Interestingly, some of these schools were evidently expanding into graduate programs, as the number of graduate students grew by 34.4 percent but remained a small share of the total.

The other two categories with smallish overall enrollment gains, the two categories of private research universities, were both close to 15 percent in aggregate growth and not much different from their public university counterparts. These two Carnegie categories experienced no institutional deaths. Similar to the previous group, these categories include the elite institutions among private research universities (though not only them), which may not have sought a great deal of enrollment growth. As might be expected, among the private research universities with "very high" research activity, graduate student numbers grew nearly twice as fast as undergraduates, +19.7 percent compared with +10.5 percent; full-time enrollments increased by 19.4 percent, while part-time enrollments *decreased* by 5.6 percent (and dropped by 33 percent for part-time undergraduates). The private research universities with high research activity are generally a less elite group than the previous category, and their graduate enrollment gains were not much more than half as large in percentage terms (+10.3 percent), while their undergraduate numbers increased by 16.9 percent. They also added full-time students in strong numbers (+26.7 percent) while shedding part-time students (−15 percent).

All the other Carnegie categories of private nonprofit colleges and universities showed healthy aggregate gains of more than 20 percent in enrollments over the eleven-year period ending in fall 2007. These aggregate gains by category ranged from 74 percent for the small category of baccalaureate/associate's schools through 45 percent for the diverse category of special focus institutions, 30+ percent for the several categories of master's institutions, around 27 percent for the sizable baccalaureate/diverse fields and the very small associate's colleges categories, and down to 21 percent for the doctoral/research university group. In general, the private nonprofit institutional categories clearly emphasizing vocational and applied fields, including at the master's degree level, have continued to prosper, as was also the case in the earlier period examined. Notably, in nearly all the Carnegie categories, the private nonprofit schools as a group achieved greater enrollment gains from 1996 to 2007 than their public sector counterparts.

As expected, the for-profit sector is not represented among the universities with high and very high research activity and is barely so in the baccalaureate arts and sciences category (many for-profit institutions are not even classified in the Carnegie scheme, especially new institutions). In the other Carnegie categories, the for-profit sector shows triple-digit and beyond percentage growth rates, but it is often built on very small baseline enrollment figures for 1996. The sector's most notable absolute gains over the recent period were in the doctoral/research university category, where enrollments burgeoned from around 5,000 in 1996 to 281,000 in 2007, a gain dominated by the

University of Phoenix and a few other multicampus for-profits that award small numbers of doctoral degrees along with many master's and other degrees. Similarly, enrollments at special focus for-profits jumped from 66,000 to 201,000, while the numbers at the master's/larger for-profit schools increased from 38,000 to 125,000. Undergraduates outnumbered graduate students in all three of these categories of rapidly growing for-profit institutions, but the share of graduate students was significant in all of them and exceeded 35 percent at the doctoral/research institutions in 2007. Finally, the category of for-profit associate's colleges, most of which also grant other kinds of postsecondary certificates and some also bachelor's degrees (but by definition less than 10 percent of all their degrees), grew impressively, from 109,000 students in 1996 to 328,000 in 2007. Unambiguously, the emphasis throughout the for-profit sector is on applied, vocationally oriented training and education.

Conclusion

In this analysis of how American private higher education sectors have fared over the last decade-plus (1996 to 2007), the private sector has generally done well in terms of the key indicators of enrollment growth and market share. As a whole, private sectors (nonprofit and for-profit together) added more than 1.5 million students and saw their share of all higher education enrollments climb from 22.7 percent to 26.1 percent over this period. This represents a near doubling of the annual enrollment growth rate for the sector from the immediately adjacent earlier period, 1980 to 1995 (Zumeta, 1999).

Important distinctions can be drawn among subsectors of the U.S. private college and university sector. First, compared to the traditional nonprofit private subsector, the for-profit sector saw more growth in numbers of students as well as—very dramatically—in percentage growth (Table 5). Particularly spectacular was the growth of the four-year (bachelor's and higher-degree-granting) for-profit sector, which added some 795,000 students, a growth rate of more than 600 percent, and increased in number of institutions from 263 to 490. Large gains occurred in graduate as well as undergraduate enrollments and in full-time as well as part-time students. Indeed, for-profit institutions enroll a large majority of students they classify as full time.

In the main, the private nonprofit sector fared reasonably well too, at least its major four-year subsector. The "flagship" private nonprofit four-year subsector added more than 670,000 students, or 23.4 percent, a growth rate nearly identical to that of public four-year institutions and greater than that of public two-year schools. Enrollment growth in this key subsector was generally well distributed across different types of institutions (by initial size and Carnegie type), with no category seeing aggregate enrollment gains much under 10 percent for the eleven-year period. As they had in the previous era (1980 to 1995), four-year private nonprofit institutions achieved their overall gains in important measure by expanding graduate programs, whose enrollments gained at a substantially greater rate (33 percent) than did undergraduate numbers (20 percent).

Notably, the pattern evident in the earlier period of emphasizing part-time students shifted as they increased only 6 percent, compared with 31 percent for full-time students. Together with the healthy gain in undergraduate numbers, it suggests that the resumption of demographic growth in traditional college-age students made it possible for many private colleges to return to their preferred emphasis on full-time students. Finally, although there was no direct analysis here of the influence of field mix on the enrollment fortunes of private institutions, the data on levels and types of students together with that on categories of institutions suggest that, broadly speaking, even in the nonprofit sector, the institutions experiencing the largest enrollment gains tended to be those emphasizing programs with an applied vocational or professional orientation. This outcome is not surprising in light of the findings of the earlier study and well-known educational and economic trends.

One caveat is necessary in evaluating how the private nonprofit sector fared in this recent period, however. The death rate of private nonprofit institutions apparently increased somewhat in the period from 1996 to 2007 compared with the period from 1980 to 1995. Although the reasons for the large numerical losses in the minuscule two-year nonprofit sector are well understood, the apparent number of institutional deaths among the four-year nonprofits (162 total and a net loss of twenty institutions over the eleven years) is considerably larger, especially on per year, than in the earlier period and may merit more detailed study using finer measures of institutional births and deaths.

In the next decade or so, it appears likely that those private nonprofit institutions lacking substantial endowments and numbers of surplus applicants will again face more challenges in maintaining their place in U.S. higher education. Numbers of traditional college-age young people are again leveling off, and more of them lack solid college preparation as well as the financial resources to readily access a private higher education. Although signs are that public sector tuitions may continue to rise as states cut back their investments in higher education, this trend may not benefit private sector competitiveness much if government student aid programs are also tightened. Moreover, for-profit institutions have proved themselves over the past decade to be very agile and market savvy. Although they are certainly reaching many students once unserved, the data indicate to some extent that these schools may be filling market niches once served or that could be served by nonprofits. The elite nonprofit institutions face no threat, but some in the middle of the pack may find themselves even more seriously squeezed than heretofore between lower-priced public competitors for traditional types of students and programs and very market- and politically astute for-profits seeking to skim the cream of potentially profitable students in applied fields that they can offer more inexpensively. This last trend especially would threaten the basic strategy that many nonprofits seem to have been pursuing with some success in recent decades.

Historically, the private nonprofit college and university sector in the United States has shown itself to be very resourceful in responding to challenges and replenishing its ranks when individual institutions have failed to survive. The sector will likely need every bit of this erstwhile leadership and resourcefulness to continue to prosper over what is likely to be a challenging decade ahead for traditional higher education.

The Private Nature of Cross-Border Higher Education

CROSS-BORDER HIGHER EDUCATION (CBHE) has not traditionally been studied as part of the private higher education universe. Nevertheless, from a regulatory perspective, it is placed with the private sector in every country that recognizes cross-border activity, even when the originating institution is part of the public sector (Lane and Kinser, 2008). From a financial perspective, too, cross-border higher education is largely tuition driven and almost never operates without the expectation of revenue surpluses (Green, Kinser, and Eckel, 2008; McBurnie and Zyguris, 2007). It also represents one aspect of broader privatization trends, where private sector initiatives and activities fill formerly exclusively state-sponsored roles. With cross-border higher education, governments promote (or at least tacitly accept) new higher education initiatives that rely substantially on nongovernment organizations to deliver the economic and educational benefits that policymakers desire.

Recent research on cross-border higher education often begins with a debate over a definitional question: What exactly is cross-border higher education? Various taxonomies have been proposed (see, for example, Becker, 2009; Vincent-Lancrin, 2007). At its broadest, cross-border higher education refers to the movement of people, projects, programs, and providers across political boundaries (Green, Eckel, Calderon, and Luu, 2007), including exchange and study-abroad programs, international branch campuses, some forms of distance education, joint-degree programs, and direct foreign ownership or investment in domestic educational institutions.

The primary responsibility for developing this chapter was taken by Kevin Kinser.

This chapter focuses on international branch campuses (IBCs) as the most prominent example of the private nature of the phenomenon. IBCs are distinguished from other forms of cross-border higher education by the physical movement of the institution from one geopolitical environment to another. Exchanges and study abroad, on the other hand, focus on the individual mobility of students and faculty. Distance education and joint-degree programs distribute the curriculum, and foreign ownership represents movement of capital. This institutional focus in examining IBCs is consistent with the broader analyses of private higher education as described in the various country cases in this volume (see especially the chapter on Dubai).

As with cross-border higher education in general, IBCs pose some definitional problems. The relationship between the home campus and the branch is at the heart of the matter, as an institution can project its image abroad in many ways, including licensing arrangements, credentialing and examination schemes, and franchise operations. Separate definitions of IBCs are provided by the Observatory for Borderless Higher Education (OBHE) (Becker, 2009) and the American Council on Education (ACE; 2009). The OBHE's definition includes "off-shore" institutions operated in the name of the home campus alone or with a domestic partner where students can earn a full degree from the foreign institution. The ACE's definition requires the branch campus to occupy educational facilities using the name of the home campus, offer courses and degrees in more than one field of study mainly through face-to-face instruction, and employ a permanent administrative staff. Although different, the definitions are similar enough to result in substantially overlapping tallies of IBCs. The OBHE, though, has traced the cross-border higher education trend over the last decade, so its definition has the advantage of longitudinal comparability. Numbers presented in this chapter generally follow the OBHE model.

The chapter begins with an overview of the trends for IBCs globally, with particular attention to several regional patterns that have emerged over the last decade. The section identifies which countries are exporting and which countries are importing. It next discusses the characteristics of IBCs, including faculty roles and curricular focus. The various financial and organizational models employed by IBCs are briefly highlighted, noting the financial implications for staffing, facilities, and academic programs. In conclusion, it presents several continuing policy and regulatory issues, along with critical assessments of the academic and organizational viability of the phenomenon.

Trends in IBCs

Much like private higher education globally, the growth in IBCs has been remarkable. The best data on numbers of campuses are provided by the OBHE (Becker, 2009; Garrett, 2002; Verbik and Merkley, 2006). The organization counted twenty-four IBCs in 2002. That number more than tripled, to eighty-two branches, by the time of the 2006 assessment and nearly doubled again, to 164 locations, in the most recent 2009 report. Although some of this numerical growth is simply the result of better data collection that comes from increased awareness of the phenomenon, the OBHE still finds that about 78 percent of the 2009 tally of IBCs were established in the past decade and that 30 percent have been initiated since the 2006 report. Moreover, the expansion came with relatively few documented failures: just eleven cases out of all branches identified by the OBHE since the mid-1990s have shut down. The closed campuses, however, offer important lessons about the limitations of the IBC concept that are discussed later in this chapter.

The patterns of growth have been distinctive as well. The 2002 OBHE report shows the dominance of Australia and the United States as IBC exporters, with eighteen of the twenty-four locations identified as coming from those two countries. By 2006 the United States was identified as the dominant exporter, with half of all the IBCs in existence at the time. The trend to this point seemed clearly in the north to south direction, with developed countries serving as the exporters to less developed countries. After 2006, however, IBCs moved sharply away from that consensus, as more north-to-north and south-to-south IBCs were identified by 2009. Still, the United States is the home country of close to half of all IBCs in the latest list, though countries such as Chile, India, Iran, Lebanon, Malaysia, Mexico, Pakistan, the Philippines, and Sri Lanka are now involved as well.

The fifty-one countries that serve as importers of IBCs can be found in Africa, Asia, Europe, the Middle East, North America, and South America. The United Arab Emirates is the leading importer, with about a quarter of all

IBCs counted in the OBHE report. The Asian countries of China and Singapore are the next most frequent destinations for IBCs, followed by Qatar, Canada, Malaysia, and the United Kingdom. The vast majority of importing countries, however, host fewer than three branches each, and only in a couple of Middle Eastern countries (the UAE and Qatar) and Singapore do IBCs represent a significant source of educational capacity.

More than a dozen countries serve as both host and source for IBCs, but the patterns here are less distinct. Canada and Malaysia host six and five IBCs, respectively, while exporting three and four. Major exporting countries—the United Kingdom, the United States. and Australia—also host a few campuses of their own, including four branches of U.S. institutions in the United Kingdom and a U.S. and a U.K. branch in Australia. Other importer-exporters include Belgium, France, Italy, Mexico, the Netherlands, Russia, South Korea, and Switzerland.

The institutional founders of IBCs are a diverse group. Comprehensive universities are the dominant source of cross-border activity, though in recent years more specialized institutions have moved into the branch campus arena. At the time of the 2002 OBHE assessment, nearly all the home campuses for IBCs were public sector institutions—except for the United States, where all were private sector institutions. In 2006 more private sector institutions from around the world opened branches, and in the United States, public sector institutions became more involved. Also at least four private for-profit institutions were operating IBCs by 2006. In the latest OBHE assessment, these trends continued. Currently, home campuses are a mix of private and public institutions, with the public sector dominating globally and private sector origins mixing in from several countries with entrepreneurial private higher education sectors. Private for-profit higher education continues to expand foreign branches, mostly represented by U.S. institutions' attempting to expand their brand abroad, along with a few other explicitly global for-profit institutions such as Malaysia's Limkokwing University and France's Vatel International Business School.

Characteristics of IBCs

Most IBCs offer a limited number of programs, commonly in business and one or two other disciplines. About 20 percent of all campuses have more comprehensive curricula available, including programs in science and technology. Programs vary by geographic region, however. The widest range of programs can be found in Europe and the Middle East. The OBHE analysis suggests that the Middle East in particular is a target for IBCs with multiple program offerings, while China (the second most popular destination for IBCs) primarily attracts business programs. Even in the Middle East, however, IBCs do not have comprehensive curricula similar to what one might find at the home campus.

A primary assumption about IBCs is that they focus on teaching to the exclusion of other activities (Altbach, 2010). True in general but with several significant exceptions, the teaching emphasis of IBCs relies on academic models that address market demand for instruction. Undergraduate programs tend to be in technical and professional fields with explicit employment prospects for graduates. From this perspective, most programs are intended to serve as terminal degrees rather than as preparation for advanced study or scholarly careers. Even so, graduate degrees are quite common in IBCs, with the master's of business administration a prominent offering. Again, the graduate degrees tend toward the technical and professional and receive relatively limited investment in independent research or scholarship at the branch campus site.

Thirteen branches, however, offer doctoral degrees, with a handful also supporting active research programs at an off-campus site. The research agenda of IBCs is often unacknowledged in the literature but represents an important goal for a subset of institutions—particularly those that emerge from research-intensive home campuses. Some host countries (China, Singapore, and several countries in the Middle East) are also beginning to see research as a significant indicator of quality branch campus initiatives and are asking branches to plan for more than instructional capacity when establishing new facilities and recruiting faculty. When campuses cannot comply, the host country may withdraw its approval to operate. The research efforts of branch campuses are not simply in response to the host country's demands, however. The United Kingdom's University of Nottingham includes significant research capacity at its branch campus in Malaysia, and U.S.-based Georgia Tech runs successful research-based Ph.D. programs at its campus in France. In both cases, the motivation for providing research at the IBC comes from the commitment of the home campus to an institutional identity as a research university.

IBCs often strain the definition of "campus" in their locations, with functional facilities devoted primarily to administrative and classroom space and limited attention to the aesthetics of campus design. Indeed many IBCs rent facilities and have made limited efforts to personalize their physical location beyond adding the home university logo to the building facade. Yet as with the Ph.D. programs at some IBCs, the counterexamples to this generalization suggest different agendas by some home institutions and host countries. Major academic cities in Dubai and Qatar suggest new IBCs may be attracted by the availability of excellent facilities. Fully developed campuses covering several hundred acres of land have been established by IBCs in Malaysia and China; in Singapore, elaborate renovations by the University of Nevada–Las Vegas created a true urban campus sited in the National Library. In a noteworthy example, the University of Nottingham replicated its famous clock tower from the home campus as an architectural focal point at each of its overseas locations. These campuses demonstrate the efforts of some IBCs to fully replicate the home campus.

Organizational and Financial Models

A key organizational feature of IBCs (and central to their inclusion in this volume) is that they are established as private entities in the host country, irrespective of their status in the home country. For public sector institutions, they thus have an identity that shifts depending on where they operate. Movement of educational services and activities outside the public institution's home geopolitical environment separates the sponsoring government from the institution, and the regulatory processes of the host government take over. It is a salient distinction between the traditional domestic education and IBCs. Using the metaphor of endemic organisms from biology, Lane and Kinser (2008) argue that the endemic organization is native to and dependent on a specific set of environmental circumstances. Leaving the home environment changes the endemic organization and creates a new, nonendemic academic institution with characteristics of both the private and public sectors. In practice, it means that public sector home institutions place financial and organizational firewalls around the branch campus that prevent mixing resources and personnel without explicit accounting. Some private sector institutions do the same thing, though others have followed a distributed organizational model that does not prioritize the home campus over the IBCs. Webster University (based in the United States), for example, encourages mobility of students and faculty across all of its campuses, and every branch site is part of a single integrated university system (Green, Kinser, and Eckel, 2008).

Working across international borders, however, does require the establishment of a new entity that is legally authorized to operate the branch (Lane, 2010b). Home institutions either set up a wholly owned subsidiary in the foreign country or work with an in-country partner through a jointly held entity. In the former case, home institutions are able to exercise the most control over branch campus operations. Not many host countries, however, allow this model. Working with a partner is therefore often a necessity rather than a choice. The partner may be a private foundation, a for-profit company, or even a government-linked entity, depending on the particular requirements and politics in the host country. The partner's motivation for getting involved with IBCs can be altruistic or self-serving. The goal could be improving educational services or opportunity for a particular region or group, or tapping into a sure revenue stream associated with IBC enrollments. In some cases, property developers have partnered with IBCs to encourage additional residential and commercial activity in the area. In this instance, the campus serves as an amenity, like a golf course or shopping center, which can increase the value of the surrounding properties.

Financially, the success of the IBC is usually measured in enrollments, not in faculty-generated research. With some notable exceptions such as those in Qatar and Abu Dhabi, IBCs tend to operate with few subsidies, and revenue from student fees must cover expenses. Without sufficient numbers of students, most IBCs would pull up stakes and go home. Some host governments subsidize the development of branch campuses or give grants and incentives to continue operating while enrollment is building. Unlike relationships of public sector institutions with their home governments, however, in a few cases such host government enticements are designed to be a permanent feature of the relationship. Alternatively, home institutions may allocate start-up costs to the branch, but in almost all cases the IBC is expected to become self-sufficient after a period of time.

The hybrid, nonendemic nature of most IBCs, combined with partner relationships and an expectation for revenue generation, suggest the complicated financial models that apply to the home institution and the branch campus. As noted above, home institutions often erect firewalls to prevent financial obligations from the branch campus from adversely affecting the main campus. The extent to which the IBC revenue is segregated, however, has various solutions. In some cases, all revenue is run through the home institution and reallocated to the branch for expenses, giving the home institution the opportunity to take a portion of the proceeds off the top to support administrative expenses. In other cases, the IBC holds its own accounts, and the home institution charges the branch for any expenses incurred. Sometimes a mix of models is used, especially when considering employment contracts. Faculty and staff may be employed by the home institution or by the branch institution and may be paid in local currency or the currency of the home country.

Finally, the academic models of the IBC depend on the organizational and financial models used to develop the branch. Tuition is linked to registration for classes, for example, so students tend to register and pay for classes through processes hosted either by the branch campus or the home campus. Degrees can be awarded by the branch campus independent of the home institution when the IBC or its partners are legally authorized to do so by the host government. The curriculum, however, is the prerogative of the home campus. IBCs may be autonomous in other areas, but when it comes to defining the programs and standards offered at remote sites, final control is clearly with the home campus.

Regulation and Policy Issues

The regulations and policy issues surrounding IBCs remain unsettled. No global authority exists for IBC activity, and government-to-government negotiations on the topic have been rare. Most countries want to maintain the right to control education provision within their borders (Lane, Brown, and Pearcey,

2004; McBurnie and Zyguris, 2007). Bilateral agreements between exporting institutions and host governments therefore create the rules of the road. Each country is different, and institutions that venture abroad must be aware of the truism that Korea is not Qatar (Green, Eckel, Calderon, and Luu, 2007; Green, Kinser, and Eckel, 2008).

By far the most pressing issue has been quality assurance (see, for example, Organization for Economic Cooperation and Development, 2005). Two dimensions apply, one relating to the home campus's risk associated with offering a low-quality program abroad and the other one involving the host country's guarding against the establishment of weak programs by low-quality IBCs. These two quality assurance problems would seem to put providers and host countries on the same page, but such is not always the case. In Malaysia, for example, efforts by the government to institute a new quality assurance regime have come into conflict with Australian IBCs' efforts to satisfy their home country's regulations on educational exports. The problem is that quality assurance remains a domestic activity around the world, and struggles to accommodate cross-border activities that are by definition international. Using the earlier metaphor of endemism, quality assurance is an endemic activity that attempts to evaluate activities of nonendemic academic institutions (Kinser, 2009). This mismatch creates a defensive posture of quality assurance border controls and places significant burdens of protection on the host country, while the home country is potentially quite aloof from on-the-ground issues that arise from exporting higher education.

The quality assurance dilemmas inherent in cross-border higher education are beginning to be addressed through regional efforts such as the European Quality Assurance Register and the Southeast Asian Quality Assurance Network. The OECD and the International Network for Quality Assurance Agencies in Higher Education are making efforts to create global standards, which aim to build consensus around the definition of quality in higher education and how it is assessed so that programs can be evaluated irrespective of national origin or destination of the institutions involved.

The issue of quality assurance reflects more narrow debates on the rules of entry into foreign countries. In particular, countries have imposed barriers to foreign ownership, limits on tuition charges, currency controls, restrictions on curricula, and demands for culturally specific content (Becker, 2009; Green, Kinser, and Eckel, 2008). Often these rules are framed as quality measures, though they are just as likely to serve as a proxy for broader policy debates that have a local political context. Malaysia, for example, has imposed various curricular and language mandates on institutions intended to protect the status of the Malay Bumiputra. India, on the other hand, has yet to agree on any regulations governing IBCs because of a national debate regarding the propriety of profit in education.

The development of education hubs is often linked with the IBC phenomenon when countries use foreign institutions to boost their educational capacity and provide educational opportunities to students their domestic systems are unable or unwilling to serve. In these cases, IBCs may be located anywhere in the country, or all of them may be located in a cluster. The first arrangement, the "archipelago hub," involves no policies limiting their locations. The second arrangement, the "acropolis hub," brings together several institutions in one location such as the Dubai International Academic City and Qatar Education City. International education hubs may involve either strategy or a combination of both. Malaysia, for example, is developing both types (Kinser and Lane, 2010).

Acropolis hubs have been the driving force behind the expansion of IBCs over the last several years. Four hubs in the UAE alone account for nearly a quarter of all IBCs in existence. Acropolis hubs have been successful in attracting IBCs because of generous tax incentives and a relaxed regulation environment. Some offer infrastructure support and administrative assistance in addition to funding student tuition and fees. Such support does not come free. Governments providing such incentives expect a return on their investment that may not match home institutions' goals or timelines. And IBCs that rely on foreign governments to balance the accounting to get off the ground may find it difficult to transition to their own resources later.

Academic freedom is also emerging as an important concern for IBCs. The major exporting countries, the United States, the United Kingdom, and Australia, all have strong traditions of academic freedom, collegial governance, and institutional autonomy. These traditions may be challenged as their institutions establish IBCs in countries with more restrictive policies—for example, acceptable limits of speech or cultural restrictions relating to religion. These topics can legitimately be considered cultural issues that should be respected when in the host country. Considering, however, that China famously censors Internet content and Middle Eastern countries have laws against homosexuality, these policies may go a step too far for home institution constituencies. One danger, of course, is the practice of self-censorship, as, for example, when an IBC changed the name of a course from U.S. Democracy to U.S. Government to avoid unwanted attention in a nondemocratic country (Green, Kinser, and Eckel, 2008, p. 20). On the other hand, some governments explicitly exempt IBCs from culturally based laws that would normally apply to citizens and residents alike. Still, acceptance of nonstandard behavior, while deemed legal in the cross-border educational environment, may still rankle local populations who see the double standard involved.

Sustainability

The sustainability of IBC activity is by no means assured. Because most IBCs are very young and policies governing the activity are not fully formed, it is difficult to determine whether more or less permanent enclaves of foreign education can be sustained. Even though relatively few IBCs have resulted in documented failures, several reasons still exist to be concerned about their future.

First, IBCs tend to be developed in an ad hoc manner. One champion emerges at the home institution and shepherds the development of the branch campus through negotiations with a champion counterpart in the host country. Generally absent are thorough market analyses and comparisons of different possible sites. The decision to expand internationally, then, is typically made in concert with the decision to establish an IBC in a particular country, which can lead to mismatches and lack of institutional commitment, especially when the champions move on to other initiatives.

Second, apart from the ad hoc nature of IBC decision making, the home campus support for establishing an overseas branch is often quite thin. Participation in the effort typically occupies only a few staff and faculty, and others on campus may be supportive only insofar as it does not affect them. At the first sign of trouble—financial difficulty, curricular controversy, quality questions—the home campus reservoir of good will could crumble and take the IBC initiative down.

A third area of concern is whether demand for IBC education is robust enough to support the number of institutions entering the market. Although most global growth in private higher education is driven by unmet demand, IBCs are also established to attract students from outside the region who have the resources to go abroad for education. In this sense, little difference exists between Dubai and Malaysia, except the cultural context where students will live. Some of the demand for IBCs in Islamic countries, in fact, comes from the perception that Western countries have become less friendly to Muslims. As the pendulum swings back, the draw of studying in the United States, as opposed to getting an "American" degree at home, may cause students to rethink their plans.

In addition, the quality of students may pose problems for institutions that are committed to providing the same curriculum abroad as at home. The pool of high-quality students may not be deep enough to support the numerous IBCs congregating in acropolis hubs. The first providers may have a head start, but the late entrants may find their reputations back home do not serve them well in recruiting talented local students.

Finally, changing policies and procedures for IBCs in the host country can quickly eliminate the incentives to participate or make it impossible to maintain home campus support for continued investments. It is an open question whether some countries seek IBCs to be long-term partners in their educational systems or see them as short-term bridges as they upgrade their domestic institutions. Advice from the American Council on Education is salient: "Know when to say when" (Green, Kinser, and Eckel, 2008, p. 21). If at the beginning of a trend a key piece of advice is to be prepared to walk away, then it should be clear that the IBC path remains hazardous.

Conclusion

IBCs represent a distinctive case of growth in private higher education. Even though home institutions are a mix of public and private sectors, the private dimensions of the IBC phenomenon are central to its development. Its trajectory and associated challenges parallel much of the private higher education literature, yet the context for IBC activity is global in scale. The rules and regulations developed to guide IBCs cross political boundaries and are still unresolved. Many institutions involved in setting up IBCs can be considered elite in their home countries, while market-driven imperatives drive curricular decisions. IBCs are not dominant in any country, though in several they make important contributions to the overall system.

IBCs are a quite small segment of the global higher education enterprise, and it is unlikely they will dominate transnational higher education. Establishing branch campuses is a resource-intensive activity, and the financial and reputational risks will give pause to most institutions. But broader globalization trends suggest that borders and geography will continue to decline in importance across a spectrum of industries. Higher education institutions will push against their traditional boundaries and expand their service areas beyond their native range. What is clear is that this expansion will occur under the regulatory mantle of private higher education, representing a new development for private higher education scholarship.

The Global Growth of Private Higher Education

$\mathbf{T}$HE COUNTRY CASES IN THIS VOLUME reinforce the introductory chapter's claim about the great interest in the growth of private higher education. The interest is logical given how spectacular the growth has been. Globally, the best estimate is that private higher education now holds 31.3 percent of total enrollments (http://www.albany.edu/dept/eaps/prophe/).

To accomplish its purposes, this concluding chapter draws on the prior chapters. But it also draws on global realities of private higher education well beyond these national cases. The varied national cases, taken together, underscore the breadth of global growth in private higher education. Some case findings provide valuable detail on what in fact are fairly typical regional and even global patterns, whereas others are more atypical; in reality, most national cases show simultaneously some atypical and some typical tendencies.

This chapter deals with five major topics: (1) a regional overview of the growth and size of private higher education; (2) the diversity of national cases in which growth occurs; (3) the diversity of types and institutions in private higher education and their attendant growth patterns; (4) the persistence of growth alongside some incidence of decline; and (5) reasons for the growth in private higher education.

Regional Overview

Two regions have experienced the greatest growth in private higher education. Latin America is 49 percent private, with Brazil the leader. Asia's private higher

The primary responsibility for developing this chapter was taken by Daniel C. Levy.

education share is 36 percent private, including more than double the raw private higher education enrollment of any other region. They are the only two regions with greater than the global average for private higher education. They are also the two where private higher education shares exceed that of the United States (26 percent). Europe (16 percent) and Africa (15 percent) trail (Levy, 2010). Definitional and other data difficulties exist in the figures for all regions, though probably least in Latin America, and further difficulties exist in comparing across regions.

In contrast to two, three, and more decades ago, the private higher education share has grown significantly in *each* region, though only for Latin America can we confidently compare it with earlier researched figures, about 34 percent in the late 1970s (Levy, 1986). Asian private higher education shares are diverse across countries, but those with longer-standing private higher education sectors tend to have the larger private higher education shares, whereas the region's soaring higher education growth has been mostly a post–World War II phenomenon (Levy, 2010). In Eastern Europe, private higher education was basically nonexistent under Communism, emerging and growing rapidly between 1990 and 1995 and then holding its own (Slantcheva and Levy, 2007); regional private higher education leaders have not grown to more than one-third private. Western Europe shows some growth in private higher education, but over recent decades only Portugal has had a major share in private higher education. Change is now occurring (Wells, Sadlak, and Vlasceanu, 2007), but most higher education privatization has involved partial privatization in public sectors. The same can be said for commonwealth countries such as Australia and Canada. Leaving aside precursors, African private higher education began in the 1980s and has grown notably, depending on country, in the last decade or two (Mabizela, Levy, and Otieno, 2007). Growth has been stronger in Anglo than Francophile countries. And in the new century, the Middle East joined the global surge; remarkable is the emergence of private higher education—largely government initiated—across most countries and a range of regimes so that the bulk of the region seems on the verge of major growth in private higher education.

A few decades ago, many countries did not allow private higher education. Now only a handful have none, and no large country is without it. Growth has been greatest in the less developed world but significant globally. Additionally, we are gauging growth by enrollment shares, whereas the private higher education share of institutions has grown even more. In east Asia, at least 90 percent of institutions are private in Japan, Indonesia, Malaysia, and the Philippines. Put another way, the growth of private higher education has produced many small institutions.

Diverse National Cases: Widespread Growth of Private Higher Education

Although the national cases covered in this volume cannot fully reflect global patterns, they do cover a wide swath. Their diversity ensures a certain breath and allows a view of the growth of private higher education in different settings. That such diverse nations would all, except the United States, have experienced at least one period of sharp growth is testimony to the reach of global growth in private higher education. The national cases have taken us to varied regional settings: Africa, Asia, Eastern Europe, and Latin America as well as the United States and cross-border settings. The growth of private higher education is widespread across large and small countries, with large and small higher education systems and private higher education shares, in developing and developed countries, and where private higher education is longstanding or only recent.

The growth of private higher education has occurred in large countries, small countries, and many in between. All other things being equal, larger countries may have larger higher education systems in terms of absolute numbers, but level of national development obviously affects higher education size. Taken together, the volume's set of countries illustrates the wide range of development settings that have seen major growth of private higher education. At the upper end is the United States, though it was a young, developing country (even colonial) when private higher education first took roots and expanded. The remaining country cases are developing countries but quite varied in that category and in size. Various cross-border arrangements show an international blend where developed countries operate in less developed countries. In Latin America, Chile, Mexico, and Brazil have been quite open to penetration, including by the for-profit Laureate network. That network accounts for a sharply increased share of Mexican higher education and private higher education enrollment. Malaysia and the United Arab Emirates are among many examples in other regions where international partners boost national private higher education. Although a private higher education presence is now almost universal, the extent of private higher education varies greatly by country. In absolute numbers, the United States remains number one. Among this volume's countries, Mexico is next. But outside the United States, the global private higher education giants are India, Brazil, Japan, Indonesia, and increasingly China. Numbers vary depending on whether one emphasizes absolute size or share of total higher education. Using shares (percentages) facilitates meaningful comparisons. Chile has easily the largest share, 78 percent, in this volume. But that amount is not so unusual if we look at east Asia, with percentages in Japan and the republic of Korea near the very top in global private higher education. Mexico also has a majority of enrollment in the private sector, but it is the only other country in this volume that does. In fact, outside Latin America, the volume's countries could give a misleading impression that small private higher education shares are the norm.

Another important variable is how early or late growth in private higher education arose. The great growth of private higher education in recent decades is such that many systems have gone from zero to a substantial share. On the other hand, other private higher education sectors are long-standing. Among this volume's cases, the United States has easily the longest-standing private higher education sector. Next is Chile, though its nineteenth-century pioneer, the Catholic University of Chile, is now only ambiguously private. The volume's youngest national private sectors, only a few decades old, are the Bulgarian and Kenyan cases, with Thailand relatively young for east Asia. The Middle Eastern cases (especially in the Gulf) are from the world's most recent national private higher education, with only scattered precursors. The cross-border sector is also a mostly recent phenomenon.

Differentiation in Private Higher Education

The breadth of growth in private higher education is shown not just by the diversity of countries but also by the diversity of private higher education in countries. The growth of private higher education is the growth of certain *types* of private higher education. Decreasingly monolithic private sectors exist, even where they sometimes first emerged as such. Intrasector differences are salient, and any ample national case study of private higher education must analyze them (Demurat, 2009; Praphamontripong, 2010).

For decades, understanding the types of growth in private higher education centered around three broad categories: religious, elite, and demand absorbing (Levy, 1986). Any sizable private higher education sector is today likely to include all three. China is a notable exception, permitting no religious institutions. In recent years, scholarship has added to and otherwise amended the three main categories. The growth of private higher education can be religious and based on group identity, elite and semielite, and poor or serious demand absorbing (Levy, 2009b). This observation is not to say that the added variants are all totally new. That statement is largely limited to for-profits, which, although probably mostly low-status demand-absorbing institutions at home, may be serious demand-absorbing institutions when part of an international operation, occasionally even bordering on semielite.

In fact, each of the three classic types and each of the fresher ones show internal differentiation. Religious and other identity institutions may attach to one group or another and be much more or less tightly affiliated with their group than their counterparts. Identity can relate to different ethnic or subnational groups. Elite and semielite can be specialized or general institutions, rather large or small. Both major types of demand-absorbing institutions can be family or business owned, domestic or international. For-profits can be tiny or part of extensive international chains. And so forth.

Even small Dubai has nonprofits and for-profits, local and more foreign management, "free zone" institutions, and differently licensed institutions. Diversity also appears in the form of IBCs in the cross-border form. This volume's Latin American cases showed little or no demand-absorbing subsectors for a long time after the emergence of private higher education but have in the last couple of decades undergone very large growth in such subsectors, including in nonuniversities.

Both in the volume's sample of countries and globally, semielite private institutions are growing. It is usually difficult to quantify this growth, as these institutions do not identify themselves as such, and the definition of them is still being designed. But a good count is possible in Thailand: the few semielite universities capture 40 percent of private higher education overall. Global growth among semielites is especially noteworthy, as more elite or world-class private higher education is very limited outside the United States. In almost every other country, the top, first choices are public. But semielite privates increasingly compete with good public universities just below the top tier.

Both in the volume's sample of countries and globally, for-profits have been emerging (Kinser and Levy, 2006). It used to be that the growth of private higher education was nonprofit growth (though many legal nonprofits operate much like for-profits). This situation has changed and there is now a mix, though nonprofit remains much more common than for-profit whether measured by enrollment or institutions. Though Chilean law does not allow for-profit universities, other higher education can be for-profit. The line between for- and nonprofit is blurry when, for example, for-profit Laureate buys up existing universities. We have also seen that for-profits have similarly been rapidly growing in Mexico—and that they constitute the fastest-growing segment of U.S. higher education. Kenya has for-profits while Thailand does not. Cross-border structures may or may not involve for-profits, but even where they do not, they usually make surplus revenue generation a principal concern.

Ongoing Growth?

Only recently has scholarly attention been given to a countertendency: the decline in private higher education (Levy, forthcoming-a). The growth of private higher education is powerful and widespread, but it is not inevitable in all situations. The rising number of public institutions had long seemed the present and future, until the current wave of privatization took hold. It is worthwhile to ponder national cases that have shown decline as well as to address the more global context.

A "decline" here means a decreased private higher education share, just as "growth" refers mostly to growth in the private higher education share. In fact, even the cases of decline in private higher education share are still few in modern times and have allowed for continued growth in absolute private enrollment.

Japan (Nagasawa, forthcoming) is the outstanding contemporary example of a fall in absolute private enrollment (while private higher education has held its share of total enrollment). Less drastic than decline can be a slowing in the rate of private higher education growth; the same factors identified as leading to a decline in private higher education can also lead to such slowing.

The most extreme form of decline in private higher education is the political abolition of the sector, but this situation is rare. Private higher education used to be commonly proscribed but it has rather infrequently been terminated. Communism brought the most dramatic examples. China had significant private higher education before communism. In Eastern Europe, the precommunist period varied with regard to the presence of private higher education.

Quite short of such extreme public termination policy, regulation sometimes tightens, posing a threat to growth in private higher education. This situation has often been the case as an initial emergence period of almost laissez-faire growth of private higher education catches government and citizens by surprise and soon becomes a matter of great concern regarding low quality, easy access, and market deception. In reaction comes "delayed regulation" (Levy, 2006). What the Bulgarian case shows in this regard has in fact been a common Eastern European pattern since the mid-1990s. Other cases of delayed or otherwise increased regulation (often involving accreditation) are discussed in the Chilean and Kenyan cases. By government command or market necessity, the prospect of private higher education institutional mergers occurs in many countries; this situation may bring a decline in private higher education enrollments but surely a direct decline in private higher education institutional share.

In other cases, the decline of private higher education shares comes fundamentally from sudden growth of the public sector. Sometimes a dramatic access opening comes in the public sector, as in Argentina in the early 1980s and the redemocratization of politics (Rabossi, 2010). Or, as in the Thai case, it may come from elevating public education institutions to higher educational status, encroaching on part of the private higher education market; the Thai private higher education share dropped from 19 to 10 percent since 1996 (Praphamontripong, 2010). In Colombia the government raised many technical institutions to higher education status (Uribe Correa, 2009).

An intriguing additional change in the public sector may also negatively affect the growth of private higher education: some public universities, striking back against the competition of the growth of private higher education, especially at the top levels, open separate units in their institutions. In many ways they are like private institutions, charging hefty tuitions and jumping into fields of study and private management previously unknown inside the public university. Such modules are common in the former Soviet Union and Asia: once the selective public quota is met, a second tier of students is admitted but to the modules. In a country like Georgia, the sum of this growth and growth in private higher education constitutes a majority of higher education enrollment. Similarly, the Bulgarian case shows that by 1997 almost half public university enrollment was in such modules. The fall of the Kenyan private higher education share from 19 percent in 2006 to 13 percent in 2004 is largely attributable to such public modules.

A "cousin" of a decline in private higher education occurs when part of private higher education becomes quite public in nature. If it remains juridically private, it technically does not fit our definition of a decline in private higher education, but functionally it comes close. Chile is a sharp historical example and unmatched by any other in the volume and few in the world. From the midtwentieth century, Chilean private higher education came to rely almost as much as public higher education on state subsidies, and distinctions in intersector governance also diminished. In much of Western Europe, nominally private institutions came to be government dependent or the like. In contrast, an increased public orientation in U.S. private higher education has been much more limited and more spread out over time and then reversed in recent decades, with much more privatization of public higher education (Morphew and Eckel, 2009).

Moreover, on the social side, demographic stagnation has already brought a decline in the private higher education share in some countries, and more is threatened. Of course, all higher education can be threatened, but private higher education (especially demand absorbing) is often more vulnerable, as it is usually not applicants' top choice. It tends to be more recent, lower status, and less legitimate as well as more expensive. The West European country with easily the largest private higher education share is the one that has most been affected by demographic decline. In Eastern Europe, the impact on private higher education has been seen more often, with a risky private higher education future in countries such as Russia. Even some Latin American and Asian private sectors face a demographic threat.

But given all these different reasons, roots, and types of decline in private higher education, one must be impressed by how subordinate a tendency it remains. And by how dominant growth continues to be.

The decline in private higher education occurs in only a small minority of cases (admittedly a bit overrepresented in this volume) and often for only short periods. The singular long-term decline in private higher education in this volume is in the United States, mostly in the third quarter of the last century and basically resulting from huge public expansion. But since that period, the U.S. private higher education share has been remarkably stable. Most countries do not appear to face an immediate threat. And in much of the developing world—where private higher education has been sharpest—population increases are still common. The very recent growth of private higher education in the Middle East is striking testimony to the continued emergence of private higher education in regions and countries previously with no or minimal private higher education. Equally dramatic is the cross-border growth in private higher education. Of course, the most decisive evidence of the growth of private higher education internationally are the global (and regional) figures reported toward the beginning of this chapter.

Additionally, private higher education has often shown resilience. In Japan significant successes have come in attracting nontraditional students (Nagasawa, forthcoming). In many countries, a decline in existing private higher education is offset by the rise of fresh forms. In Kenya the rise of evangelical institutions is an example. In the United States, the most striking example is the growth of for-profit institutions.

Explaining the Growth in Private Higher Education

The key reasons for growth in private higher education have long been established (Levy, 1986). They have proved strikingly durable across time and varied circumstances. The classic causes relate to the private higher education types discussed above. Of course, the weight of causes varies by type of private higher education.

Whereas Catholic identity has weakened as a cause of growth in private higher education, other religious and ethnic identities have grown. Whereas the seeking of an academic or quality or social advantage has been a relatively weak factor outside the Americas, it is rising in the semielite subsector. But the biggest shift among the traditional explanations of growth is the overwhelming prevalence today of demand-absorbing factors. The crux is that soaring demand for higher education greatly exceeds existing (mostly public) supply. In turn, the soaring demand has been the result of demographic growth, economic expansion, a rising middle class, rising social aspirations, and expanding labor markets (Cao, 2007); in turn the labor-market orientation has shaped the business-related fields that have sharply characterized private higher education in nearly all our cases. The only exception among this volume's cases is the United States, though its for-profit subsector does fit the global generalization. Most of the growth factors in private higher education have been sharpest in the developing world, where demand-absorbing realities have been strongest. And many of the same factors explain the noteworthy demand met by local and international for-profits.

Laying aside the growth of different private higher education types, several other factors often bring growth to the private higher education sector overall. Socioeconomic development and a growing middle class have been crucial. Here, however, the focus is on further *political* perspectives on the expansion of private higher education in general, first highlighting regimes and broad political-economic policy and then more particular higher education policies.

The most dramatic regime change in this volume is the (imposition and then) demise of communism in Bulgaria. As in the region overall, private higher education could rocket from near zero to a notable presence. For the regime, it was mostly about shifting from proscription to permission, though also about the shift from a command economy to a market economy's bringing new demands to higher education, demands often suitable to the emerging private sector. In contrast, regime changes in Chile have not produced the same decisive private-public changes in higher education. The 1973 military coup led to repression and other changes but not to a starkly proprivate growth policy until a decade and more later. Noteworthy was that the 1990 redemocratization did not bring fundamental shifts with regard to private-public in higher education. Little civilian thirst existed (even on the left) to reverse course and undermine the private tendencies.

Less dramatic than regime change were significant shifts in political-economic policies in regimes. In recent decades, in this volume's cases and beyond they have mostly involved a more open, market-oriented economy— and privatization. Such was the case for Thailand, Kenya, and Mexico, though the advent of democracy and rightist party presidential victory in Mexico in 2000 did not mean drastic reversals of economic or higher education policy. But in the last decade or so, private higher education shares have slipped in both Kenya and Thailand, so one must be wary of assuming simple numerical correlations when it comes to market orientation and growth in private higher education shares of total higher education. In both Kenya and Thailand and other countries, the partial privatization in public higher education is a complicating variable. In Dubai and most of the Middle East, a confounding variable is the blurring of public and private, particularly given the heavy role of government in creating private higher education, much more so than in any other region; at the same time, the opening of the region's economies is an instrumental factor in the emergence and growth of private higher education. Cross-border initiatives have also signaled Middle Eastern and other openings.

Although the United States has not experienced the magnitude of political-economic change that other countries have, it has undergone intensified privatization in the economy and in higher education. In comparative terms, it has moved from a public sector more private than in most countries and to more private in finance and management than it had been. Again, however, a rapid growth of private higher education share is not the result. What does grow rapidly is the for-profit private higher education subsector.

Apart from broad political-economic changes, public policy can promote (or inhibit) the growth of private higher education in many ways. Sometimes the intention is to promote; sometimes promotion is just a by-product. Most obvious in intention to promote is public policy to allow private higher education; a corollary is permission to allow for-profit sectors or certain cross-border forms. Among policies that generally promote private higher education without an explicit plan to do so are tuition charges for public institutions. Higher public tuition reduces the "tuition gap" between private and public sectors and therefore is favorable to the growth of private higher education. (The volume's cases reflect a rise of public sector tuition but also overrepresent the tendency. The sharpest cases here are Chile and the United States.) A notable recent development for high public sector tuition was discussed earlier, in the creation of privatized modules in public universities.

Striking for its near absence (in this volume and in most of the world) is growth of private higher education through public policy of direct, regular subsidies to private higher education (Levy, forthcoming-b; Pachuashvili, forthcoming). With the exception of Chile historically and some Western European countries, public funding of private higher education resembling its funding of public higher education is extremely rare. More common but still rare is any annual subsidization of private higher education institutions. In this volume, for example, this generalization is illustrated in Bulgaria and Mexico. The United States is exceptional in some of its states, though never does the direct funding of the private sector match that of the public sector.

But the United States leads the way in other financial policy very supportive of the growth of private higher education (Zumeta, forthcoming). Especially if one focuses on federal policy, it concerns "sector neutrality." That is, important funding streams are given without regard to whether the beneficiary is public or private. Research grants are instead based on judgments of merit. Student loans are based on student need so long as students enroll at accredited institutions. A remarkable and perhaps distinctive U.S. policy is the inclusion of for-profits for the student loans; for-profit private growth would not be nearly what it is were there not such government financial support. For all its private proclivities, Chile does not open student funding fully to private higher education. Thailand, on the other hand, is sector neutral on such funding. China has just become so, and growth of private higher education is part of the purpose. The World Bank favors such sector neutrality, again partly to boost the growth of private higher education.

The growth of private higher education is not a result simply of national public policy, however. We have seen fresh international and cross-border polices as well as the Bologna process. And most of all, we have seen the growth of private higher education as the result of many private and individual "policies."

Notes

1. Based on 2009 exchange rate.
2. For this analysis, we use the eight standard census regions used by the U.S. Census Bureau: *New England*—Connecticut, Maine, Massachusetts, New Hampshire, Rhode Island, Vermont; *Mideast*—Delaware, District of Columbia, Maryland, New Jersey, New York, Pennsylvania; *Great Lakes*—Illinois, Indiana, Michigan, Ohio, Wisconsin; *Plains*—Iowa, Kansas, Minnesota, Missouri, Nebraska, North Dakota, South Dakota; *Southeast*—Alabama, Arkansas, Florida, Georgia, Kentucky, Louisiana, Mississippi, North Carolina, South Carolina, Tennessee, Virginia, West Virginia; *Southwest*—Arizona, New Mexico, Oklahoma, Texas; *Rocky Mountains*—Colorado, Idaho, Montana, Utah, Wyoming; *Far West*—Alaska, California, Hawaii, Nevada, Oregon, Washington.
3. The categories are (1) associate's colleges (fourteen subcategories by sector and setting), (2) baccalaureate colleges (arts and sciences), (3) baccalaureate colleges (diverse offerings), (4) baccalaureate colleges (associate's as well as bachelor's offerings), (5) master's colleges and universities (larger programs), (6) master's colleges and universities (medium programs) and master's colleges and universities (smaller programs), (7) doctoral/research institutions, (8) research universities (high research activity), (9) research universities (very high research activity), and (10) special focus institutions.

References

Abagi, O., Nzomo, J., and Otieno, W. (2005). *Private higher education in Kenya.* Paris: UNESCO/IIEP.

Abdullah, M. M. (1978). *The United Arab Emirates: A modern history.* London: Croom Helm Press.

Ajayi, J.F.A., Goma, K. H., and Johnson, A. G. (1996). *The African experience with higher education.* Accra, Athens, and London: Association of African Universities, Ohio University Press, and James Curry.

Altbach, P. G. (2005). Universities: Family style. In P. G. Altbach and D. C. Levy (Eds.), *Private higher education: A global revolution* (pp. 29–32). Rotterdam, The Netherlands: SensePublishers.

Altbach, P. G. (2010). Why branch campuses may be unsustainable. *International Higher Education, 58,* p. 2.

Altbach, P. G., Reisberg, L., and Rumbley, L. (2009). *Trends in global higher education: Tracking an academic revolution.* Chestnut Hill, MA: Center for International Higher Education, Boston College.

American Council on Education. (2009, September). U.S. branch campuses abroad. ACE Issue Brief. Washington, DC: American Council on Education.

American University in Dubai. (2009). AUD fact sheet, 2009. Retrieved July 12, 2010, from http://www.aud.edu/about_aud/files/AUDFactSheet.pdf.

Asociación Nacional de Universidades e Instituciones de Educación Superior. (2001). *Anuario estadístico, 2001.* México DF: Asociación Nacional de Universidades e Instituciones de Educación Superior.

Asociación Nacional de Universidades e Instituciones de Educación Superior. (2002). *Anuario estadístico, 2002.* México DF: Asociación Nacional de Universidades e Instituciones de Educación Superior.

Asociación Nacional de Universidades e Instituciones de Educación Superior. (2003a). *Anuario estadístico, 2003.* México DF: Asociación Nacional de Universidades e Instituciones de Educación Superior.

Asociación Nacional de Universidades e Instituciones de Educación Superior. (2003b). *Mercado lboral de profesionistas en Mexico. Diagnostico (1990–2000), Primera Parte.* Mexico DF: Asociación Nacional de Universidades e Instituciones de Educación Superior.

Asociación Nacional de Universidades e Instituciones de Educación Superior. (2006). *Anuario estadístico, 2006.* México DF: Asociación Nacional de Universidades e Instituciones de Educación Superior.

Balán, J., and Garcia de Fanelli, A. M. (1997). El sector privado de la educación superior. In R. Kent (Ed.), *Los temas críticos de la educación superior en América Latina. Vol. 2: Los años 90. Expansión privada, evaluación y posgrado* (pp. 9–93). México DF: Fondo de Cultura Económica.

Becker, R. (2009). *International branch campuses: Markets and strategies.* London: Observatory on Borderless Higher Education.

Bernasconi, A. (2003). Private higher education with an academic focus: Chile's new exceptionalism. *International Higher Education, 32,* 18–19.

Bernasconi, A., and Fernández, E. (2008). Das sterben privater universitäten in Chile. *Die Hochschule, 17*(2), 71–83.

Boonprasert, M. (2002). Private higher education in Thailand *The report of the Second regional seminar on private higher education: Its role in human resource development in a globalised knowledge society* (pp. 119–128). Bangkok, Thailand: SEAMEO-RIHED.

Boyadjieva, P. (2003, October). *University models and social change: American university model as a factor for democratization of the Bulgarian society.* Paper presented at the seventh joint conference of North American and Bulgarian scholars, The Ohio State University, Columbus.

Boyadjieva, P., and Slantcheva, S. (2007). Public perceptions of private universities and colleges in Bulgaria. In S. Slantcheva and D. C. Levy (Eds.), *Private higher education in postcommunist Europe: In search of legitimacy* (pp. 223–238). New York: Palgrave Macmillan.

Brunner, J. J. (1986). *Informe sobre la educación superior en Chile.* Santiago de Chile: FLACSO.

Brunner, J. J., and Uribe, D. (2007). *Mercados universitarios: El nuevo escenario de la educación superior.* Santiago: Ediciones Universidad Diego Portales.

Bureau of Legal Affairs. (2007). *Goht maay lamdap rong tee aawk tam kwam nai Prarachabanyat Sathabun Udomsuksa Akachon B.E. 2546* [Supplementing Regulations of Private Higher Education Act 2003]. Compilation of procedural regulations. Bangkok, Thailand: Office of the Commission on Higher Education.

Bureau of Policy and Planning. (2003). *Sam todsawat tabuang mahawitthayalai* [Three decades: The Ministry of University Affairs]. Bangkok, Thailand: Office of the Commission on Higher Education.

Cao, Y. (2007). *Chinese private colleges and the labor market.* Doctoral dissertation, State University of New York at Albany.

Chaloemtiarana, T. (1979). *Thailand: The politics of despotic paternalism.* Bangkok, Thailand: Social Science Association of Thailand and Thai Khadi Institute, Thammasat University.

Chapman, B. (2005). *Income contingent loans for higher education: International reform* (Vol. 491). Canberra, Australia: Centre for Economic Policy Research, Research School of Social Sciences, Australian National University.

Chongwibul, P. (2001). *The roles of private universities in Bangkok Metropolitan and vicinities in managing higher education.* Master's thesis, Mahidol University, Bangkok.

College Board. (2008a). Trends in college pricing. Retrieved July 12, 2010, from www .collegeboard.com/trends.

College Board. (2008b). Trends in student aid. Retrieved July 12, 2010, from www.college board.com/trends.

Comisión Nacional de Acreditación. (2008). Informe resultados acreditación, 2008. Retrieved July 12, 2010, from http://www.cnachile.cl/docs/Informeacreditacion2008. pdf.

Commission on Academic Accreditation. (2010). Active institutions. Retrieved January 10, 2010, from http://www.caa.ae/caa/DesktopModules/Institutions.aspx.

Croom, P. (2010). Motivations and aspirations for international branch campuses. In D. W. Chapman and R. Sakamoto (Eds.), *Cross border collaborations in higher education: Partnerships beyond the classroom.* New York: Routledge.

Darling, F. C. (1962). American policy in Thailand. *Western Political Quarterly, 15*(1), 93–110.

Davidson, C. M. (2008). *Dubai: The vulnerability of success.* New York: Columbia University Press.

Davidson, C. M., and Smith, P. M. (Eds.). (2008). *Higher education in the Gulf states: Shaping economies, politics, and culture.* London: Saqi Books.

Demurat, J. (2008). *The first-second choices: What methods do ambitious Polish private higher education institutions use to attract near pinnacle students?* Paper presented at the 33rd Annual Conference of the Association for the Study of Higher Education, International Division, November 5–8, Jacksonville, Florida.

Demurat, J. (2009). *The first-second choices: What methods do Polish private higher education institutions use to attract students?* Paper presented at the 53rd Annual Conference of the Comparative and International Education Society, March 22–26, Charleston, South Carolina.

Department of Economic and Social Affairs, Population Division. (2009). Expat numbers rise rapidly as UAE population touches 6m. Retrieved July 12, 2010, from http://uaeinteract.com/docs/Expat_numbers_rise_rapidly_as_UAE_population_touches_6m/37883 .htm.

Dubai International Academic City. (2010). DIAC leading education service provider according to UNESCO report on universities in Arab countries. Retrieved July 12, 2010, from http://www.diacedu.ae/media-room.php/DIAC/9.

Dubai Statistics Center. (2008). Statistical Yearbook. Dubai: Author.

Dubai Statistics Center. (2010). Population clock. Retrieved January 10, 2010, from http://www.dsc.gov.ae/en/pages/home.aspx.

Eurydice. (2007). *Key data on higher education in Europe.* Brussels, Belgium: European Commission.

Eurydice. (2009). *Key data on education in Europe*. Brussels, Belgium: European Commission.

Excelencia Free Zone. (2008). *UEA Free Zone Investment Guide* (2nd ed.). United Arab Emirates: Excelencia FZ LLC.

Fineman, D. (1997). *A special relationship: The United States and military government in Thailand, 1947–1958*. Honolulu: University of Hawaii Press.

Fisher, D., and others. (2004). *Market ideology and educational policy in Canadian higher education: The changing boundary between the public and private sectors in British Columbia, Ontario, and Québec, 1990–2003.* Paper presented at the CHER 17th Annual Conference: Public-Private Dynamics in Higher Education—Expectations, Developments, and Outcomes, September 17–19, University of Twente, the Netherlands.

Friedman, T. L. (2000). *Understanding globalization: The Lexus and the olive tree*. New York: Anchor Books.

Garrett, R. (2002). *International branch campuses: Scale and significance*. London: Observatory on Borderless Higher Education.

Geiger, R. L. (1985). The private alternative in higher education. *European Journal of Education, 20*(4), 385–398.

Geiger, R. L. (1986). *Private sectors in higher education: Structure, function, and change in eight countries*. Ann Arbor: University of Michigan Press.

Geiger, R. L. (1991). Private higher education. In P. G. Altbach (Ed.), *International higher education: An encyclopedia* (Vol. 1, pp. 233–246). New York: Garland Publishing.

Gellert, C., and Rau, E. (1992). Diversification and integration: The vocationalisation of the German higher education system. *European Journal of Education, 27*(1/2), 89–99.

Gill, J. (2008, August 21). Oiling the learning machine. *Times Higher Education*. Retrieved July 12, 2010, from http://www.timeshighereducation.co.uk/story.asp?storycode=403223.

Goodman, R., and Yonezawa, A. (2007). Market competition, demographic change, and educational reform: The problems confronting Japan's private universities in a period of contraction. In J. Enders and B. Jongbloed (Eds.), *Public-private dynamics in higher education: Expectations, developments and outcomes* (8th ed., pp. 443–470). Bielefeld, Germany: Transcript Verlag.

Green, M. F., Eckel, P. D., Calderon, L., and Luu, D. T. (2007). *Venturing abroad: Delivering U.S. degrees through overseas branch campuses and programs*. Washington, DC: American Council on Education.

Green, M. F., Kinser, K., and Eckel, P. D. (2008). *On the ground overseas: U.S. degree programs and branch campuses abroad*. Washington, DC: American Council on Education.

HCT Factbook. (2009). Retrieved November 22, 2009, from http://www.hct.ac.ae/facts Nfigures/aspx/factsfigures_09.aspx.

Hussey, A. (1993). Rapid industrialization in Thailand, *1986–1991. Geographical Review, 83*(1), 14–28.

Johnstone, B. (2009). Worldwide trends in financing higher education: A conceptual framework. Retrieved September 9, 2009, from http://www.gse.buffalo.edu/org/IntHigherEd Finance/project_publications.html.

Kamunge, J. M. (1988). *Report of the presidential working party on education and manpower training for the next decade and beyond (Kenya)*. Nairobi: Government of Kenya.

Kelly, K. F. (2001). *The rise of for-profit degree-granting institutions: Policy considerations for states*. Denver: Education Commission of the States.

Kenya National Assembly. (1986). *Economic management for renewed growth*. Nairobi: Government of Kenya.

Kinser, K. (2006). *From Main Street to Wall Street: The transformation of for-profit higher education*. San Francisco: Jossey-Bass.

Kinser, K. (2007). Dimensions of corporate ownership of for-profit higher education. *Review of Higher Education, 30*(3), 217–245.

Kinser, K. (2009). Liberalisation, quality, and profit: Tensions in cross border delivery of higher education. Paper presented at the Global Higher Education Forum, December 13, Penang, Malaysia. Retrieved July 12, 2010, from http://www.gheforum.usm.my/2009/doc/preghef/Kevin Kinser_State Univ of New York Albany.pdf.

Kinser, K. (2010). A global perspective on for-profit higher education. In W. G. Tierney, V. M. Lechuga, and G. Hentschke (Eds.), *For-profit colleges and universities: Their markets, regulation, performance, and place in higher education* (pp. 145–170). Sterling, VA: Stylus Press.

Kinser, K., and Lane, J. E. (2010). Deciphering "educational hubs" strategies: Rhetoric and reality. *International Higher Education, 59*, 18–19.

Kinser, K., and Levy, D. C. (2005). The for-profit sector: U.S. patterns and international echoes in higher education. *PROPHE Working Paper No. 5*. Retrieved July 12, 2010, from http://www.albany.edu/dept/eaps/prophe/publication/paper/PROPHEWP05_files/PROprivate higher educationWP05.pdf.

Kinser, K., and Levy, D. C. (2006). For-profit higher education: United States tendencies, international echoes. In J.J.F. Forest and P. G. Altbach (Eds.), *International handbook on higher education* (pp. 107–120). New York: Springer.

Knowledge and Human Development Authority. (2010). KHDA listing. Retrieved July 12, 2010, from www.khda.gov.ae.

Kolasiński, M., Kulig, A., and Lisiecki, P. (2003). The strategic role of public relations in creating the competitive advantages of private higher education in Poland: The example of the School of Banking in Poznań. *Higher Education in Europe, 28*(4), 433–447.

Kruss, G. (2002). More, better, different? Understanding private higher education in South Africa. *Perspectives in Education, 20*(4), 15–28.

Kruss, G. (2007). Credentials and mobility: An analysis of the profile of students choosing to study at registered private higher education institutions in South Africa. In M. Mabizela, D. C. Levy, and W. Otieno (Eds.), *Journal of Higher Education in Africa. Special Issue: Private Surge amid Public Dominance: Dynamics in the Private Provision of Higher Education in Africa, 5*, 135–154.

Kulachol, T. (1995). Private higher education in Thailand. In T-I Wongsothorn and W. Yibing (Eds.), *Private higher education in Asia and the Pacific: Final report. Part II: Seminar papers* (pp. 109–127). Bangkok, Thailand: UNESCO PROAP and SEAMEO-RIHED.

Kwiek, M. (2007). The European integration of higher education and the role of private higher education. In S. Slantcheva and D. Levy (Eds.), *Private higher education in post-communist Europe: In search of legitimacy* (pp. 119–134). New York: Palgrave Macmillan.

Kwiek, M. (2008). The two decades of privatization in Polish higher education: Cost-sharing, equity, and access. *Die Hochschule. Journal für Wissenschaft und Bildung, 2,* 94–112.

Kwiek, M. (2009). *Equitable access to higher education and European integration: New public-private dynamics.* Paper presented at the international workshop, Towards a European Higher Education Area: Bologna Process and Beyond, March 7, University of Michigan, Ann Arbor.

Lane, J. E. (2010a). *Higher education, free zones, and quality assurance in Dubai* (Policy Paper). Dubai School of Government.

Lane, J. E. (2010b). Joint ventures in cross-border higher education: International branch campuses in Malaysia. In D. W. Chapman and R. Sakamoto (Eds.), *Cross border collaborations in higher education: Partnerships beyond the classroom* (pp. 67–91). London: Routledge.

Lane, J. E. (forthcoming). Importing private higher education: International branch campuses. *Journal of Comparative Policy Analysis.*

Lane, J. E., Brown, M.C.I., and Pearcey, M.-A. (2004). Transnational campuses: Obstacles and opportunities for institutional research in the global education market. *New Directions for Institutional Research, 124,* 49–62.

Lane, J. E., and Kinser, K. (2008). The private nature of cross-border higher education. *International Higher Education, 53,* 11.

Laothamatas, A. (1992). *Business associations and the new political economy of Thailand: From bureaucratic polity to liberal corporatism.* Boulder, CO: Westview Press.

Levy, D. C. (1986). *Higher education and the state in Latin America: Private challenges to public dominance.* Chicago: University of Chicago Press.

Levy, D. C. (2002). Unanticipated development: Perspectives on private higher education's emerging roles. *PROPHE Working Paper No.1.* Retrieved July 12, 2010, from http://www.albany.edu/dept/eaps/prophe/publication/paper.html.

Levy, D. C. (2005). Conclusion: Observations from the field. In G. A. Philip and D. C. Levy (Eds.), *Private higher education: A global revolution* (pp. 283–292). Rotterdam, The Netherlands: SensePublishers.

Levy, D. C. (2006). The unanticipated explosion: Private higher education's global surge. *Comparative Education Review, 50*(2), 218–240.

Levy, D. C. (2007a). Legitimacy and privateness: Central and Eastern European private higher education in global context. In S. Slantcheva and D. C. Levy (Eds.), *Private higher education in postcommunist Europe: In search of legitimacy.* New York: Palgrave Macmillan.

Levy, D. C. (2007b). *Private-public interfaces in higher education development: Two sectors in sync?* Paper presented at the Conference on Higher Education and Development, the 2007 World Bank Regional Seminar on Development Economics, January 16–17, Beijing, China.

Levy, D. C. (2007c). Public money for private higher education. *International Higher Education, 49,* 14.

Levy, D. C. (2007d). A recent echo: African private higher education in an international perspective. *Journal of Higher Education in Africa. Special Issue: Private Surge amid Public Dominance: Dynamics in the Private Provision of Higher Education in Africa, 5*, 197–220.

Levy, D. C. (2008a). *Exploring the viability of a semi-elite category.* Paper presented at the 33rd Annual Conference of the Association for the Study of Higher Education, International Division, November 5–8, Jacksonville, Florida.

Levy, D. C. (2008b). Indian private higher education in comparative perspective. *PROPHE Working Paper No. 13.* Retrieved July 12, 2010, from http://www.albany.edu/dept/eaps/prophe/publication/paper.html.

Levy, D. C. (2009a). *The decline of private higher education.* Paper presented at the 18th Annual Forum of the ASHE Council on International Higher Education, November 5, Vancouver, BC.

Levy, D. C. (2009b). Growth and typology. In S. Bjarnason and others (Eds.), *A new dynamic: Private higher education* (pp. 1–28). Paris: UNESCO.

Levy, D. C. (2010). *East Asian private higher education: Reality and policy.* Washington, DC: World Bank Flagship Project on East Asia.

Levy, D. C. (forthcoming-a). The decline of private higher education? *PROPHE Working Paper.* Retrieved July 12, 2010, from http://www.albany.edu/dept/eaps/prophe/publication/paper.html.

Levy, D. C. (forthcoming-b). Public policy for private higher education: A global analysis. In D. C. Levy and W. Zumeta (Eds.), *Journal of Comparative Policy Analysis.*

Mabizela, M. (2003). *Consolidating resources and managing growth? Challenges and roles of private providers of higher education in sub-Saharan Africa.* Paper presented at the International Conference hosted by the United States International University on Meeting the Challenges of Higher Education in Africa: The Role of Private Universities, September 3–5, Nairobi, Kenya.

Mabizela, M., Levy, D. C., and Otieno, W. (Eds.). (2007). Private surge amid public dominance: Dynamics in the private provision of higher education in Africa. *Special issue: Journal of Higher Education in Africa, 5*(2/3).

Maldonado, A. (2002). El banco mundial y la educación superior en los países en desarrollo ¿cuáles son los peligros y las promesas. In F. Lopez (Ed.), *Educación superior latinoamericana y organismos internacionales. Un análisis crítico* (pp. 167–185). Cali, Colombia: Universidad de San Buenaventura, UNESCO, Boston College.

Matawatsarapak, P. (2001). Sathaban satsana Christ nikai Roman Catholic kub parakijtangkansuksa nai prated Thai. Unpublished research paper. Bangkok, Thailand: Social Science Research Center, Research Institute, Assumption University.

McBurnie, G., and Zyguris, C. (2007). *Transnational education: Issues and trends in offshore higher education.* London: Routledge.

McCargo, D., and Pathmanand, U. (2005). *The thaksinization of Thailand.* Copenhagen, Denmark: Nordic Institute of Asian Studies Press.

Mei, T. A. (2002). *Malaysian private higher education: Globalization, privatization, transformation, and marketplaces.* London: ASEAN Academic Press.

Morphew, C. C., and Eckel, P. D. (2009). *Privatizing the public university: Perspectives from across the academy.* Baltimore: Johns Hopkins University Press.

Mwiria, K., and Ng'ethe, N. (2002). *Public University Reform in Kenya: Mapping the Key Changes of the Last Decade.* Unpublished Research Report.

Mwiria, K., and others. (2007). *Public and private universities in Kenya: New challenges, issues, and achievements of education.* Nairobi and Oxford: East African Educational Publishers and James Currey.

Nagasawa, M. (forthcoming). *Institutional differentiation in Japanese private higher education: Key dimensions of diversified social functions.* Doctoral dissertation, State University of New York at Albany.

National Statistical Institute. (2009). Database. Retrieved September 9, 2009, from http://www.nsi.bg/SocialActivities_e/Education_e.htm.

National Statistical Institute. (2010). Database. Retrieved June 11, 2010, from http://www.nsi.bg/otrasal.php?otr=23.

Neave, G., and van Vught, F. (1994). Government and higher education in developing nations: A conceptual framework. In G. Neave and F. van Vught (Eds.), *Government and higher education relationships across three continents: The winds of change* (Vol. 2, pp. 1–21). Oxford: International Association of Universities and Elsevier Science Ltd.

Ntshoe, I. M. (2004). Higher education and training policy and practice in South Africa: Impacts of global privatization, quasi-marketization and new managerialism. *International Journal of Educational Development, 24*, 137–154.

Nyaigoti-Chacha, C. (2004, August). *Reforming higher education in Kenya: Challenges, lessons, and opportunities.* Paper presented at the SUNY Parliamentary Education Committee Workshop, Education, Science and Technology in Kenya, Naivasha.

Onsongo, J. (2007). The growth of private universities in Kenya: Implications for gender equity in higher education. In M. Mabizela, D. C. Levy, and W. Otieno (Eds.), *Journal of Higher Education in Africa. Special Issue, Private Surge amid Public Dominance: Dynamics in the Private Provision of Higher Education in Africa. 5,* 111–134.

Organization for Economic Cooperation and Development. (2005). UNESCO/OECD guidelines: Quality provision in cross-border higher education. Retrieved July 12, 2010, from http://www.oecd.org/document/52/0,3343,en_2649_39263238_29343796_1_1_1_1,00.html.

Organization for Economic Cooperation and Development. (2009). Tertiary education in Chile. In *Reviews of National Policies for Education.* Paris: Organization for Economic Cooperation and Development.

Otieno, W. (2002). *In between the master and the mammon? Privatizing trends and challenges in Kenyan higher education.* Paper presented at the Program for Research on Private Higher Education, November 7, State University of New York at Albany.

Otieno, W. (2003). *Financing higher education for increased access amid the politics of public-private partnerships: The Kenyan experience.* Paper presented at the workshop, The Role of Higher Education Loan Boards in Enhancing Access and Equity in Higher Education, April 9, Kenya School of Monetary Studies.

Otieno, W. (2004). Student loans in Kenya: Past experiences, current hurdles, and opportunities for the future. *Journal of Higher Education in Africa, 2*(2), 75–99.

Otieno, W., and Levy, D. C. (2007). *Public disorder, private boons? Intersectoral dynamics illustrated by the Kenyan case.* PROPHE Working Paper No. 9. Retrieved July 12, 2010, from http://www.albany.edu/dept/eaps/prophe/publication/paper.html.

Pachuashvili, M. (2008). Private-public dynamics in postcommunist higher education. *Die Hochschule. Journal für Wissenschaft und Bildung, 2,* 84–93.

Pachuashvili, M. (forthcoming). Governmental policies and their impact on private higher education development in post-Communist countries. In D. C. Levy and W. Zumeta (Eds.), *Journal of Comparative Policy Analysis.*

Penkov, B. (1992). Bulgarian higher education. In B. Clark and G. Neave (Eds.), *The encyclopaedia of higher education* (pp. 95–99). Oxford: Pergamon Press.

Phongpaichit, P., and Baker, C. (2002). *Thailand economy and politics* (2nd ed.). New York: Oxford University Press.

Phongpaichit, P., and Baker, C. (2004). Aftermath: Structural change and policy innovation after the Thai crisis. In K. S. Jomo (Ed.), *After the storm: Crisis, recovery, and sustaining development in four Asian economies* (pp. 150–172). Singapore: Singapore University Press.

Popov, N. (2001). A review of higher education reform in Bulgaria. *International Higher Education, 23,* 27–28.

Praphamontripong, P. (2008a). Inside Thai private higher education: Exploring private growth in international context. PROPHE Working Paper No. 12. Retrieved July 12, 2010, from http://www.albany.edu/dept/eaps/prophe/publication/paper.html.

Praphamontripong, P. (2008b). *Institutional governance and finance of semielite private universities: What differences do they bring to the Thai higher education system?* Paper presented at the 33rd Annual Conference of the Association for the Study of Higher Education, International Division, November 5–8, Jacksonville, Florida.

Praphamontripong, P. (2010). *Intrasectoral diversity: A political economy of Thai private higher education.* Doctoral dissertation, State University of New York at Albany.

Rabossi, M. A. (2010). Universities and fields of study in Argentina: A public-private comparison from the supply and demand side. PROPHE Working Paper No. 15. Retrieved July 12, 2010, from http://www.albany.edu/dept/eaps/prophe/publication/paper.html.

Radev, T. (2009). *Short-cycle study programs within the system of higher education in Bulgaria.* Paper presented at the international conference, Recognition and Accreditation of Short-Cycle Higher Education Programs in Europe and the United States: Aligning Educational Systems, June 15–17, Varna, Bulgaria.

Ranking de Universidades 2008. (2008, November). *Qué pasa,* pp. 8–20.

Rauhvargers, A., Deane, C., and Pauwels, W. (2009). Bologna Process: Stocktaking report. Retrieved September 9, 2009, from http://www.ond.vlaanderen.be/hogeronderwijs/bologna/conference/documents/Stocktaking_report_2009_FINAL.pdf.

Reisz, R. D. (2003). Public policy for private higher education in Central and Eastern Europe: Conceptual clarifications, statistical evidence, open questions.

HoF Arbeitsberichte. Institute for Higher Education Research at the Martin Luther University Halle. Halle-Wittenberg, Germany: Wittenberg University.

Rodríguez, E. (2009). Rendición de cuenta pública de la Comisión Nacional de Acreditación. Retrieved July 12, 2010, from http://www.cnachile.cl/docs/cuentapublica-corr-3.pdf.

Secretaría de Educación Pública. (2000). *Acuerdo 279 trámites y procedimientos relacionados con el reconocimiento de validez oficial de estudios del tipo superior:* Mexico City: Diario Oficial de la Federación.

Secretaría de Educación Pública. (2008). Estadística histórica del sistema educativo nacional. Retrieved July 12, 2010, from http://www.dgpp.sep.gob.mx/Estadi/NACIONAL/index.htm.

Serrano, S. (1994). *Universidad y nación: Chile en el siglo XIX.* Santiago, Chile: Editorial Universitaria.

SESIC. (2004). *Aspectos financieros del sistema universitario de educación superior:* México DF: Secretaría de Educación Pública.

Silas Casillas, J. C. (2005). Recognizing the subsectors in Mexican private higher education. *International Higher Education, 40,* 13–14.

Silas Casillas, J. C. (2008). *Almost there: Semielite private institutions in Mexico.* Paper presented at the 33rd Annual Conference of the Association for the Study of Higher Education, International Division, November 5–8, Jacksonville, Florida .

Slantcheva, S. (2007a). Bulgaria. In P. Wells, J. Sadlak, and L. Vlasceanu (Eds.), *The rising role and relevance of private higher education in Europe* (pp. 63–100). Bucharest, Romania: UNESCO-CEPES.

Slantcheva, S. (2007b). Legitimating the difference: Private higher education institutions in Central and Eastern Europe. In S. Slantcheva and D. Levy (Eds.), *Private higher education in postcommunist Europe: In search of legitimacy* (pp. 55–74). New York: Palgrave Macmillan.

Slantcheva, S., and Levy, D. C. (Eds.). (2007). Private higher education in post-Communist Europe: In search of legitimacy. New York: Palgrave Macmillan.

Swan, M. (2010, February 3). Women dominate first crop of UAE PhD students. Retrieved February 5, 2010, from http://www.thenational.ae/apps/pbcs.dll/article?AID=/20100203/NATIONAL/702029805/1001/REVIEW.

Swaroop, S. (2004, December 2/). Adopting a progressive approach. *Gulf News.*

Trow, M. A. (1987). The analysis of status. In B. R. Clark (Ed.), *Perspectives on higher education: Eight disciplinary and comparative views* (pp. 132–164). Berkeley and Los Angeles: University of California Press.

United Arab Emirates University. (2008). Emirates University factbook, 2007–2008. Retrieved November 20, 2009, from http://www.uaeu.ac.ae/irpsu/factbook/2007–2008/chapter1.pdf.

Uribe Correa, L. (2009). *The decline of private higher education in Colombia: Causes and consequences?* Paper presented at the 18th Annual Forum of the ASHE Council on International Higher Education, November 4–5, Vancouver, BC.

U.S. Bureau of the Census. (2007). *Current population survey: Annual social and economic supplements. Tables P-15 and P-16.* Washington, DC: Economics and Statistics Administration, U.S. Department of Commerce,

Verbik, L., and Lasanowski, V. (2007). *International student mobility: Patterns and trends.* London: Observatory on Borderless Higher Education.

Verbik, L., and Merkley, C. (2006). *The international branch campus: Models and trends.* London: Observatory on Borderless Higher Education.

Villa, L., and Flores-Crespo, P. (2002). Las universidades tecnológicas en el espejo de los institutos universitarios de tecnología franceses. *Revista mexicana de investigación educativa, 7*(14), 17–49.

Vincent-Lancrin, S. (Ed.). (2007). Cross-border tertiary education: A way towards capacity development. Paris: Organization for Economic Cooperation and Development/World Bank.

Watson, K. (1991). Thailand. In P. G. Altbach (Ed.), *International higher education: An encyclopedia* (Vol. 1, pp. 559–578). New York: Garland Publishing.

Weisbrod, B. (1977). *The voluntary nonprofit sector: An economic analysis.* Lexington, MA: Lexington Press.

Wells, P. J., Sadlak, J., and Vlasceanu, L. (2007). *The rising role and relevance of private higher education in Europe.* Bucharest, Romania: UNESCO-CEPES.

Wilkins, S. (2001). Human resource development through vocational education in the United Arab Emirates: The case of Dubai Polytechnic. *Journal of Vocational Education & Training, 54*(1), 5–26.

World Bank. (1985). *Sub-Saharan Africa: From crisis to sustainable growth.* Washington, DC: World Bank.

World Bank. (2000). *Higher education in developing countries: Peril and promise.* Washington, DC: World Bank.

World Bank. (2001). Educational statistics. Retrieved September 9, 2009, from http://devdata.worldbank.org/edstats.

World Bank. (2002). *Constructing knowledge societies: New challenges for tertiary education.* Washington, DC: International Bank for Reconstruction and Development.

World Bank. (2005). *Bulgaria – Education and Skills for the Knowledge Economy.* Washington, DC: International Bank for Reconstruction and Development.

World Bank. (2007). *Accelerating Bulgaria's convergence: The challenge of raising productivity Vol. 2.* Washington, DC: World Bank.

Zayed University. (2009). *Enrollment Data.* Retrieved August 2, 2010 from http://www.caa.ae.

Ziderman, A. (2003). *Student loans in Thailand: Are they effective, equitable, sustainable?* Vol. 1. Bangkok, Thailand: UNESCO/ IIEP.

Ziderman, A. (2006). Student loans in Thailand: From social targeting to cost sharing. *International Higher Education, 42,* 6–8.

Zumeta, W. (1992). State policies and private higher education: Policies, correlates, and linkages. *Journal of Higher Education, 63*(4), 363–417.

Zumeta, W. (1996). Meeting the demand for higher education without breaking the bank: A framework for design of state higher education policies for an era of increasing demand. *Journal of Higher Education, 67*(4), 367–425.

Zumeta, W. (1999). *How did they do it? The surprising enrollment success of private, nonprofit higher education from 1980 to 1995.* IHELG Monograph 99-9. Houston: Institute for Higher Education Law and Governance, University of Houston Law Center.

Zumeta, W. (2005). Accountability and the private sector: State and federal perspectives. In J. Burke and Associates (Eds.), *Achieving accountability in higher education: Balancing public, academic, and market demands* (pp. 25–54). San Francisco: Jossey-Bass.

Zumeta, W. (forthcoming). State policies and private higher education in the USA: Understanding the variation. In D. C. Levy and W. Zumeta (Eds.), *Journal of Comparative Policy Analysis. Special issue.*

Name Index

A
Abagi, O., 53
Abdullah, M. M., 65
Altbach, P. G., 44, 83, 111

B
Baker, C., 78, 80
Balán, J., 13–14
Becker, R., 64, 72, 107, 108, 109, 116
Bernasconi, A., 29
Boonprasert, M., 77
Boyadjieva, P., 43, 50
Brown, M.C.I., 114–115
Brunner, J. J., 24, 26, 30

C
Calderon, L., 107, 115
Cao, Y., 130
Chaloemtiarana, T., 77
Chapman, B., 86
Chongwibul, P., 82
College Board, 93
Croom, P., 63, 74

D
Darling, F. C., 77
Davidson, C. M., 67, 69
Deane, C., 42
Demurat, J., 82, 125

E
Eckel, P. D., 107, 113, 115, 116, 117,
    118, 128
Eurydice, 42

F
Fernández, E., 29
Fineman, D., 77
Fisher, D., 90
Flores-Crespo, P., 11
Friedman, T. L., 78, 80

G
Garcia de Fanelli, A. M., 13–14
Garrett, R., 109
Geiger, R. L., 37, 43, 83
Gellert, C., 83
Georgievi, E., 43
Georgievi, H., 43
Gill, J., 68
Goodman, R., 24
Green, M. F., 107, 113, 115, 116, 117, 118

H
Hussey, A., 77

J
Johnstone, B., 39

K
Kazim, A., 73
Kelly, K. F., 94
Kinser, K., 1, 2, 6, 11, 74, 83, 94, 97, 107,
    112, 113, 115, 116, 117, 118, 126
Kolasinski, M., 48–49
Kruss, G., 55
Kulachol, T., 77, 78, 84
Kulig, A., 48–49
Kwiek, M., 38, 39

Subject Index

A

Academic entrepreneurship, in Mexico, 11
Accreditation: in Bulgaria, 40–41; in Chile, 30, 32; in Dubai, 40–41; in Kenya, 40–41
Aga Khan University, in Kenya, 58
America University of Dubai, 69, 72–73, 75
American Council on Education (ACE), 108
Argentina, and private higher education, 127
Arsomsilp Institute of the Arts and Development (Thailand), 81
Asociación Nacional de Universidades e Instituciones de Educación Superior, 10
Assumption University (Thailand), 89
Austral University in Valdivia (Chile), 25

B

Bangkok College (Thailand), 77
Bangkok University (Thailand), 82
Birla Institute of Technology and Science–Pilani (Dubai), 73
Bologna process, influence of, 41
Branch campuses, in Dubai, closure of, 75
British University of Dubai, 68
Bulgaria's private higher education, 6, 37–50; Bologna process, 41; College for Islamic Studies, 47; Council of Rectors, 47; delayed regulation, 48; demand-absorbing institutions, 45; diversification, 42; enrollments, 41; expansion of private institutions, 37–39; Free University of Sofia, 43; funding, 42;

higher education system, 39–42; legislative framework, 44–45; National Evaluation and Accreditation Agency, 40–41; New Bulgarian University, 44; organizational forms, 44; part-time faculty from state universities, 48–49; post-communism transformation of Bulgarian higher education system, 39–40; public policy, 47–49; semielite institutions, 45–47; Slavic University in Sofia, 43; state and private institutions (table), 46; student-teacher ratios, 42; tuition fees, 41
Bureau of Legal Affairs, 85
Bureau of Policy and Planning, 77

C

Canadian University of Dubai, 68
Catholic universities, 130; in Chile, 24–25, 31; in Mexico, 13
Catholic University of Eastern Africa (CUEA), 55, 56, 58–59
Catholic University of Valparaíso (Chile), 25
CBHE, See Cross-border higher education (CBHE)
Chile's private higher education, 5–6, 23–35; accreditation, 30, 32; Austral University in Valdivia, 25; Catholic University, 24–25, 31; Catholic University of Valparaíso, 25; Council of Higher Education (Ministry of Education), 29; Council of Rectors, 31, 34; delayed

E

Eastern Europe, and private higher education, 127

Enrollments, 1, 6, 91–94; in Bulgaria, 37–38, 40–41, 41, 49; in Chile, 24, 26–28, 31, 24; in Dubai, 66, 71–75; and global growth of private higher education, 121–124, 126–128; international branch campuses (IBCs), 113; in Kenya, 54–55, 59–60, 62; in Mexico, 9–19; patterns, in American private education sectors, 97–104; in Thailand, 78, 80, 82–83, 89

Europe, expansion of private institutions across, 43–47

European Quality Assurance Register, 115

Excelencia Free Zone, 69

Exeter University in Dubai, 68

Expansion of private institutions: in Bulgaria, 37–39; in Europe, 43–47

F

Federico Santa María Technical University (Chile), 25

Financing, in Kenya, 60–61

Free University of Sofia (Bulgaria), 43

Free zones, in Dubai, 64–65, 69–71, 70–71

G

Growth frameworks, in Mexico, 12–14

H

HCT Factbook, 66

High school enrollment, in Mexico, 10

Higher Colleges of Technology (HCT), in Dubai, 65–66

Higher education, global growth of, 7

Hult University (Dubai), 68

I

IBCs, *See* International branch campuses (IBCs)

Income-contingent loans, in Thailand, 86–87

INSEAD, 68

Integrated Postsecondary Education Data System (IPEDS), 92, 96, 98

International Academic City (Dubai), 64, 69–70, 116

International branch campuses (IBCs): and academic freedom, 116–117; acropolis hubs, 116; American Council on Education (ACE), 108; archipelago hubs, 116; characteristics of, 110–112; defined, 108; enrollments, 113; growth patterns, 109; importers of, 109–110; key organizational feature of, 112; Observatory for Borderless Higher Education (OBHE), 108; organizational and financial models, 112–114; regulation and policy issues, 114–117; sustainability, 117–118; trends in, 109–110

International Network for Quality Assurance Agencies in Higher Education, 115

International Standard Classification of Education (ISCED), 42

Islamic and Arabic Studies College (IASC), 67–69

Islamic and Buddhist colleges, in Thailand, 81

J

Japan, and private higher education, 127

K

Kenya's private higher education, 6, 51–53; Aga Khan University, 58; Catholic University of Eastern Africa (CUEA), 55, 56, 58–59; Daystar University, 55, 58; diversification, 58–60, 59–60; elite vs. nonelite private higher education, 57–58; financing, 60–61; growth of , 51–62; Kenyatta University, 54; Kiriri Women's University of Science and Technology (KWUST), 56–57; Legal Notice No. 56 (The Universities Standardization, Recognition, and Supervision Rules), 53; loan

University of the Thai Chamber of Commerce (Thailand), 82
University of Wollongong in Dubai (UOWD), 67, 75
University Quality Assurance International Board (UQAIB), 70–71
U.S. Bureau of the Census, 93, 100

W

World Bank, 38, 42, 45, 87, 89

Z

Zayed University (Dubai), 65–67

About the Authors

Kevin Kinser is associate professor of educational administration and policy studies and co–team leader of the Cross-Border Education Research Team at the State University of New York at Albany. He is a collaborating scholar of the Program for Research on Private Higher Education. His research interests include the organization and regulation of for-profit higher education.

Daniel C. Levy is distinguished professor in educational administration and policy studies at the State University of New York at Albany. He is director of the Program for Research on Private Higher Education. His main interest is how educational institutions fit into the interface between civil society and the state.

Juan Carlos Silas Casillas is associate professor at the Department of Education of ITESO, Guadalajara's Jesuit University. He holds a Ph.D. in higher education from the University of Kansas and is an affiliate of the Program for Research on Private Higher Education. His scholarly interests and production are focused on private higher education in Mexico and Latin America as well as organizational issues in higher education settings.

Andrés Bernasconi is associate professor and provost at Universidad Andrés Bello. He is a collaborating scholar of the Program for Research on Private Higher Education and principal researcher of the Program for Research on Higher Education Policy. His research interests in higher education include regulation, organizational structure, and the academic profession.

Snejana Slantcheva-Durst is assistant professor of higher education at the University of Toledo in Ohio. She is a collaborating scholar of the Program for Research on Private Higher Education, contributing research and publications on private higher education in Central and Eastern Europe.

Wycliffe Otieno is currently chief of education with UNICEF in Papua, New Guinea. Previously a lecturer at Kenyatta University, he is an affiliate of the Program for Research on Private Higher Education. His major area of scholarship is higher education, with a keen interest in finance, privatization, and equity.

Jason E. Lane is assistant professor of educational administration and policy studies and co–team leader of the Cross-Border Education Research Team at the State University of New York at Albany. His research focuses on government oversight, accountability, and cross-border education. As a Fulbright New Century Scholar, he studied international branch campuses throughout the Gulf and Middle East.

Prachayani Praphamontripong is an affiliate of the Program for Research on Private Higher Education at the State University of New York at Albany. Her research interests include private higher education, private-public distinction, private-public partnerships, organizational studies, organizational leadership, institutional governance and finance, public policy, quality assurance and accreditation, and internationalization of higher education.

William Zumeta is professor of public affairs and higher education at the University of Washington–Seattle and president of the Association for the Study of Higher Education. His research interests include higher education policy and finance as well as the relationships between public policies and private sectors of higher education.

Robin LaSota is a CREST Fellow and Ph.D. student in educational leadership and policy studies at the University of Washington's College of Education. Her research focuses on policies and practices that improve outcomes and strengthen transitions between pre-K–12 and postsecondary education.

About the ASHE Higher Education Report Series

Since 1983, the ASHE (formerly ASHE-ERIC) Higher Education Report Series has been providing researchers, scholars, and practitioners with timely and substantive information on the critical issues facing higher education. Each monograph presents a definitive analysis of a higher education problem or issue, based on a thorough synthesis of significant literature and institutional experiences. Topics range from planning to diversity and multiculturalism, to performance indicators, to curricular innovations. The mission of the Series is to link the best of higher education research and practice to inform decision making and policy. The reports connect conventional wisdom with research and are designed to help busy individuals keep up with the higher education literature. Authors are scholars and practitioners in the academic community. Each report includes an executive summary, review of the pertinent literature, descriptions of effective educational practices, and a summary of key issues to keep in mind to improve educational policies and practice.

The Series is one of the most peer reviewed in higher education. A National Advisory Board made up of ASHE members reviews proposals. A National Review Board of ASHE scholars and practitioners reviews completed manuscripts. Six monographs are published each year and they are approximately 120 pages in length. The reports are widely disseminated through Jossey-Bass and John Wiley & Sons, and they are available online to subscribing institutions through Wiley InterScience (http://www.interscience.wiley.com).

Call for Proposals

The ASHE Higher Education Report Series is actively looking for proposals. We encourage you to contact one of the editors, Dr. Kelly Ward (kaward@wsu.edu) or Dr. Lisa Wolf-Wendel (lwolf@ku.edu), with your ideas.

The Global Growth of Private Higher Education

Recent Titles

ORDER FORM SUBSCRIPTION AND SINGLE ISSUES

DISCOUNTED BACK ISSUES:

Use this form to receive 20% off all back issues of *ASHE Higher Education Report.*
All single issues priced at **$23.20** (normally $29.00)

TITLE	ISSUE NO.	ISBN

Call 888-378-2537 or see mailing instructions below. When calling, mention the promotional code JBNND to receive your discount. For a complete list of issues, please visit www.josseybass.com/go/aehe

SUBSCRIPTIONS: (1 YEAR, 6 ISSUES)

☐ New Order   ☐ Renewal

U.S.	☐ Individual: $174	☐ Institutional: $265
CANADA/MEXICO	☐ Individual: $174	☐ Institutional: $325
ALL OTHERS	☐ Individual: $210	☐ Institutional: $376

Call 888-378-2537 or see mailing and pricing instructions below.
Online subscriptions are available at www.onlinelibrary.wiley.com

ORDER TOTALS:

Issue / Subscription Amount: $ _____

Shipping Amount: $ _____
(for single issues only – subscription prices include shipping)

Total Amount: $ _____

SHIPPING CHARGES:
First Item $5.00
Each Add'l Item $3.00

(No sales tax for U.S. subscriptions. Canadian residents, add GST for subscription orders. Individual rate subscriptions must be paid by personal check or credit card. Individual rate subscriptions may not be resold as library copies.)

BILLING & SHIPPING INFORMATION:

☐ **PAYMENT ENCLOSED:** *(U.S. check or money order only. All payments must be in U.S. dollars.)*

☐ **CREDIT CARD:** ☐VISA ☐MC ☐AMEX

Card number _____Exp. Date_____

Card Holder Name_____Card Issue # _____

Signature _____Day Phone_____

☐ **BILL ME:** *(U.S. institutional orders only. Purchase order required.)*

Purchase order # _____
Federal Tax ID 13559302 • GST 89102-8052

Name _____

Address_____

Phone_____ E-mail_____

Copy or detach page and send to: **John Wiley & Sons, PTSC, 5th Floor**
989 Market Street, San Francisco, CA 94103-1741

Order Form can also be faxed to: **888-481-2665**

PROMO JBNND